Check for:
1 DVD

KITCHEN MAKEOVERS
FOR ANY BUDGET

CHRIS GLEASON

B
BETTERWAY HOME
CINCINNATI, OHIO
www.fwmedia.com

Read This Important Safety Notice

To prevent accidents, keep safety in mind while you work. Use the safety guards installed on power equipment; they are for your protection.

When working on power equipment, keep fingers away from saw blades, wear safety goggles to prevent injuries from flying wood chips and sawdust, wear hearing protection and consider installing a dust vacuum to reduce the amount of airborne sawdust in your woodshop.

Don't wear loose clothing, such as neckties or shirts with loose sleeves, or jewelry, such as rings, necklaces or bracelets, when working on power equipment. Tie back long hair to prevent it from getting caught in your equipment.

People who are sensitive to certain chemicals should check the chemical content of any product before using it.

Due to the variability of local conditions, construction materials, skill levels, etc., neither the author nor Popular Woodworking Books assumes any responsibility for any accidents, injuries, damages or other losses incurred resulting from the material presented in this book.

The authors and editors who compiled this book have tried to make the contents as accurate and correct as possible. Plans, illustrations, photographs and text have been carefully checked. All instructions, plans and projects should be carefully read, studied and understood before beginning construction.

Prices listed for supplies and equipment were current at the time of publication and are subject to change.

Metric Conversion Chart

to convert	to	multiply by
Inches	Centimeters	2.54
Centimeters	Inches	0.4
Feet	Centimeters	30.5
Centimeters	Feet	0.03
Yards	Meters	0.9
Meters	Yards	1.1

KITCHEN MAKEOVERS FOR ANY BUDGET. Copyright © 2010 by Chris Gleason. Printed and bound in China. All rights reserved. No part of this book may be reproduced in any form or by any electronic or mechanical means including information storage and retrieval systems without permission in writing from the publisher, except by a reviewer, who may quote brief passages in a review. Published by Betterway Home Books, an imprint of F+W Media, Inc., 4700 East Galbraith Road, Cincinnati, Ohio, 45236. First edition.

Distributed in Canada by Fraser Direct
100 Armstrong Avenue
Georgetown, Ontario L7G 5S4
Canada

Distributed in the U.K. and Europe by David & Charles
Brunel House
Newton Abbot
Devon TQ12 4PU
England
Tel: (+44) 1626 323200
Fax: (+44) 1626 323319
E-mail: postmaster@davidandcharles.co.uk

Distributed in Australia by Capricorn Link
P.O. Box 704
Windsor, NSW 2756
Australia

Visit our Web site at www.popularwoodworking.com.

Other fine Popular Woodworking and Betterway Home Books are available from your local bookstore or direct from the publisher.

14   13   12   11   10   5   4   3   2   1

Library of Congress Cataloging-in-Publication Data

Gleason, Chris, 1973-
   Kitchen makeovers for any budget / by Chris Gleason.
      p. cm.
   ISBN 978-1-55870-882-2 (pbk. : alk. paper)
   1. Kitchens--Design and construction. 2. Kitchens--Remodeling.
I. Title.
   TH4816.3.K58G54 2010
   643'.3--dc22
                                    2009040679

ACQUISITIONS EDITOR: David Thiel, david.thiel@fwmedia.com
SENIOR EDITOR: Jim Stack, jim.stack@fwmedia.com
DESIGNER: Brian Roeth
PRODUCTION COORDINATOR: Mark Griffin
PHOTOGRAPHER: Chris Gleason
ILLUSTRATOR: Jim Stack

About the Author

 Chris Gleason has owned and operated Gleason Woodworking Studio for a decade. A self-taught craftsman, he specializes in contemporary furniture and kitchens.

With a degree in French from Vassar College in Poughkeepsie, New York, Chris had the opportunity to live and study abroad for a year in Switzerland. The mountain influence must have grabbed hold, as he now makes his home in Salt Lake City, Utah, where he mountain bikes and skis as much as possible. He is also an enthusiastic old-time banjo and fiddle player.

Chris is the author of *Built-In Furniture for the Home, Old-School Woodshop Accessories, The Complete Custom Closet, Building Real Furniture for Everyday Life* and he's presently writing a book about designing and building outdoor furniture and accessories.

About the Author

Although my business tackles a wide range of projects, kitchens have become more and more central to my daily work. By being immersed in kitchen design, construction and installation, I've learned a great deal, and I would like to thank my clients for providing me with the opportunities to do so.

These essential collaborations provide the creative spark that drives my never-ending quest to master a very complex set of challenges — crafting a kitchen that looks great and works well — a lofty goal indeed! This book represents the sum of the lessons I've learned, and, hopefully it will be helpful to those who are thinking about undertaking kitchen projects of their own.

I'd also like to offer my sincere thanks to both Jim Stack and David Thiel at F+W Media for helping to make this book a reality. Jim does an incredible job in giving form to the chaotic mass of documents and pictures that I hand him, and David trusts me enough to let me follow inspiration where it leads. Together, I think we've created an attractive and useful reference book.

And last but not least, I wish to thank my wonderful wife, Michele, who manages to somehow be exuberant and steadfast at the same time. The world needs more people like her.

CONTENTS

SECTION 01

7 INTRODUCTION

9   A Look at Today's Kitchens

10   A Word About Kitchen Trends

13   Interview with Ingrid Becker of Arendal Design

14   Interview with Paul Becker of Arendal Design

16   Attention to Detail

16   Drawer Slides Are Not Created Equal

17   A Word About Dovetailed Drawers

18   Planning Your Hood Fan

20   Interview with Jesse Spencer from Gygi Culinary Environments

24   Interview with Seth Striefel

26   Interview with Appliance Specialist Troy Haney from Mountainland Design Culinary & Bath Environments

28   Spotlight on Appliances

32   Types of Mouldings and Trims

36   Kitchen Design Details

38   Universal Design

39   Spotlight on Countertops

SECTION 02

41 MAKING IT YOUR OWN

41   Introduction and Planning: Where Do You Start?

42   Money-Saving Strategies

43   Putting It All Together

46   Quiz #1: Assessing Your Current Kitchen

47   Quiz #2: Planning for Your New Kitchen

48   Quiz #3: What's It Going to Cost?

49   Resale

49   And Now for the Data

50   Paying for the New Kitchen

50   Scheduling Tips

51   The Work Triangle, Diamond and Beyond

51   Island Design

54   Small-Kitchen Planning

55   Spotlight on Cabinetry

56   Layout

58   Floor Plans

63   Basic Kitchen Specifications

63   Kid-Friendly Kitchen Design

64   Corner-Cabinet Layout

68   Getting It On Paper

SECTION 03

71 DO IT YOURSELF

72 A DIY Remodeling Success Story

77 Top-Notch Organizers at a Reasonable Price

78 Tiling a Backsplash

80 Cabinet Refacing

81 Cabinet Construction

81 Building Cabinets in Production Runs

86 Designing and Building Drawers

90 Finishing Cabinet Drawers

92 Pull-Out Pantry Design and Construction

97 Cabinet Doors and Drawer Fronts
with Continuous Horizontal Grain

101 Hanging Wall Cabinets

SECTION 04

103 CASE STUDIES

103 Szykula Kitchen

113 Christensen Kitchen

127 Bohner Kitchen

133 Broadmoor Kitchen

138 Thinking Beyond the Kitchen:
Using Adjacent Spaces

143 Suppliers

INTRODUCTION

Remodeling a kitchen is one of the most daunting tasks that most homeowners will ever undertake. A major obstacle is the lack of a road map to help them understand how the process works. Contrary to the hearsay, half-truths and horror stories that most of us have heard, remodeling a kitchen doesn't have to be a painful ordeal. If you start by describing exactly what you want and develop a plan for it, then you can create the kitchen of your dreams in a fairly civilized manner. You'll know how much time to allot for demolition and when to schedule a plumber. You'll know which jobs to tackle on your own and which to leave to the pros. The whole process can go smoothly, and, if you hit some bumps in the road, you'll be better prepared to get past them quickly and easily. Having an understanding of the entire process will allow you to better manage it day-by-day. This book provides a detailed look at the process of designing, building and installing kitchens from the ground up.

This book is organized into four sections: from looking at kitchen design in general to specific strategies you can use in planning your own project. You'll learn how to efficiently lay out the cabinetry and appliances, provide adequate and accessible storage and draft a lighting plan that will create an attractive and functional impact.

I discuss the pros and cons of the latest materials and trends and help you hone in on the details that will make your project exactly what you want it to be. There's chapter for woodworkers that details how you can save a ton of money by building and installing your own cabinets.

The book wraps up with a series of case studies showing how I planned and created kitchens for my own clients. It's my hope that these will provide you with some useful ideas as you move ahead with your own kitchen plans.

I've presented a lot of step-by-step information that is thorough enough to guide a do-it-yourselfer through the nitty-gritty of an entire remodel — while at the same time recognizing the needs of the many people who may never pick up a hammer but still want a guide for planning and decision-making. It's my hope this book will help you organize your kitchen project with greater expertise and confidence.

CHRIS GLEASON • SALT LAKE CITY, UTAH • MARCH 2008

01
A LOOK AT TODAY'S KITCHENS

Introduction

Figuring out where to start can sometimes be the hardest part of planning your new kitchen. We live in a time where you have more choices than ever before, and that can be overwhelming. I firmly believe that good kitchen planning is rooted in two things: Evaluating your needs and wants and having a good understanding of your options in meeting them.

This section will set the stage for your remodel by exploring the overall process. Included are:

- A survey of the latest trends in hardware, organization and style
- Strategies for smart appliance shopping so you can get the most for your money
- Interviews with design professionals who, collectively, have decades of design experience

A Word About Kitchen Trends

My experience is that few people want to be right on the cutting edge of a brand new trend — there is something nerve-racking about wondering if your design choices are going to feel outdated in a couple of years, so playing it safer can feel more comfortable.

Most of my clients talk about designs that will endure and age well, but this doesn't mean that they're afraid to try new things or make some bold choices. Most of my clients are willing to embrace new ideas that enhance functionality, such as drawer-style dishwashers and convection ovens, but they are more hesitant when it comes to over-the-top materials such as zebrawood veneers for cabinetry or polished concrete floors.

In the end, all of the options, whether they're functional or aesthetic in nature, are a matter of personal taste. Regardless of what you decide for yourself, I am a big advocate of being educated about the options. With this in mind, I've compiled a list of recent kitchen trends.

RECENT TRENDS
- Mixing and matching styles is popular and creates calculated eclecticism
- Open storage is not limited to upper cabinets but includes the ends of islands
- Great-room kitchens that are open to other rooms, (i.e. family rooms, etc.)
- Highly-articulated hearth areas
- Inexpensive wall brackets supporting open shelves is an opportunity to create notable aesthetic impact
- Displaying collections in hard-to-reach areas that you don't need to access often

CABINETRY DESIGN AND LAYOUT
- Wall cabinets that continue down onto countertops are not just for appliance garages
- Appliance garage door styles using lift-up hardware, etc.
- Cubby designs are a great way to break up blocky-looking or uninspired cabinet layouts
- Distressing can work with certain styles
- Mixing color schemes could be just a center island that is set apart in terms of color/finish/style
- Furniture styles applied to cabinets are not always on every cabinet, just key ones
- Varied heights on upper cabinets
- The white-on-white kitchen is likely to endure
- An island with a cutout and two sliding baskets within will break up the linear design of the cabinets

SPOTLIGHT ON MATERIALS

Backsplashes:
- Tile offers a lot of options
- Whole wall of tile (not just below the cabinets)
- Beadboard is a wooden element that can tie in with the cabinets and create a solid, built-in look
- Pressed tin and other vintage looks
- A place to store utensils. You can have them exposed and convenient (which might look cluttered) or down-to-earth and homey

Flooring:
- Cork is easy on the feet
- Bamboo is a sustainable product but it is shipped from Asia
- Forbo — original linoleum
- Hardwood (it can be sealed for day-to-day use)
- Low-maintenance: What color of hardwoods hide dirt the best?
- A bachelor friend of mine installed a beautiful travertine floor in his kitchen, which works fine for him, but in my home, where there are dogs, cats and kids, a more dirt-hiding material might work better

A SURVEY OF NEW HARDWARE OFFERINGS

Should you go for the latest bells and whistles? In my experience, probably not. If you look through the catalogs of the companies that produce kitchen organizers and accessories, it can seem like overkill for those of us with more down-to-earth lifestyles. I'm reasonably organized by nature, and I don't need to be excruciatingly detailed about keeping the tongs separate from the spatulas, so a lot of the new gizmos would just be wasted on me. That said, I think there are a lot of neat items out there that can help people feel at home and be productive in their new kitchens, so it's worth taking a look.

One of the most notable trends is the soft-close concept. It began a few years ago with drawer slides and has now expanded to manufacturers that offer European-style hinges with integrated soft-close mechanisms. These systems offer several advantages:

1. No loud bangs when doors and/or drawers are slammed shut.
2. No more drawers that don't close all the way — this is one of my pet peeves.
3. Smoothly operating drawers that close themselves is one of life's little luxuries.

Soft-close drawer slides and hinges cost a bit more, but that makes up a small percentage of the average remodeling budget. Are they worth it? In my opinion, yes. This technology is quickly trickling down from the high-end of the market, and, in a few years, it will probably be the standard for mid-range kitchens.

Rockler's soft-close adapter attaches to your present kitchen drawers and works with the hardware already installed.

If you're thinking about resale value of your home, I recommend spending the extra money here.

If you're re-facing a kitchen, you may want to look at a new product that Rockler is offering: It's a roller-runner soft-close adapter for under $6 per drawer.

Blum's Servo-Drive system is the first, to my knowledge, to offer self-opening drawers for base cabinets. The appeal lies in the fact that you can open drawers when your hands are full. With a slight nudge, the drawer will glide open. The system incorporates a concealed electric drive unit, and it certainly belongs in the luxury category, as it adds about $150 to the cost of a drawer. I can see this being used in settings where adaptive design principles apply. (For example, people who have trouble grasping traditional drawer pulls would find this system useful.)

Both Blum and Salice, two major manufacturers of cabinet hardware, have introduced systems for wall cabinets that allow the doors to open upward. The styles are suited to contemporary kitchens, but they offer such convenient access to the contents of a cabinet that I'm sure they will be utilized in kitchens of varying styles as time goes on.

If you're the kind of person who wants a place for everything and everything in its place, you will like the latest generation of organizer and accessories. You can mix and match a huge variety of gadgets to create the storage solutions that best suit your needs. You'll often hear of such compound setups referred to as "super cabinets".

It appears that the manufacturers of kitchen organizers have thought of just about everything. Even though few people go hog wild and outfit entire kitchens with the latest and greatest accessories, I always encourage my clients to flip through a catalog or two because there are some clever ideas that can help you to get the most out of your new kitchen.

Blum's Servo-Drive is a hands-free drawer-opening system.

The Aventos HL hardware is easy to open, can be stopped at any desired position and closes silently and effortlessly.

Here's a cooking center with everything literally at your fingertips.

ACCORDING TO *CABINETMAKER*
MAGAZINE, APRIL 2008:
What's hot today?
- Dark finishes, with light finishes a close second
- Maple and cherry woodwork
- Clever storage options
- Islands
- Solid surface countertops with a new look, i.e., engineered quartz
- Doors with cleaner lines and less fussy embellishments
- Open shelving
- Stainless steel cooktop hoods
- Stainless steel appliances

What's in the future?
- Oak — rift-sawn or quartersawn
- Light-colored cabinets will overtake dark cabinets
- Much more lighting
- Green approach will become stronger
- Creative-looking countertops will increase
- Upper cabinets replaced by shelves (or gone altogether)
- More drawer appliances

Base-cabinet storage in a corner can be accomplished in a number of creative ways.

INTERVIEW WITH INGRID BECKER OF ARENDAL DESIGN

I spoke with Ingrid Becker of Arendal Design, who has over 30 years of experience as a kitchen designer. Because of her deep background in the field, she had an interesting perspective, not simply on today's attitudes and trends, but also on the history of kitchen design of the past few decades.

She observed that people seemed to be trend-focused in their design sensibilities until about 10 or 15 years ago. At that point, she noted a fundamental shift in the way her clients approached the process. Rather than adhering to specific styles, people started feeling a bit more liberated in their tastes. The prevailing attitude came to reflect a desire to "do what pleases you" and to make your kitchen design a personal statement. This philosophy has endured to the present day and manufacturers have shifted gears to offer a broad range of options for a public with diverse and individualized preferences.

Even in the face of a design culture which encourages individuality more than ever, Ingrid noted that there are still some trends at work, with some of them appearing to be shaped by forces on a much broader scale. For example, the events of 9-11 (the destruction of the Twin Towers in New York City) marked a profound shift not only in our national mindset but also in the way we feel about our homes. As Americans dealt with the social and political uncertainty of those times, many people strived to establish their homes as safe, secure oases.

Ingrid noted that her clients' tastes became more anchored in traditional styles for several years afterward. As time passed, however, and the American economy surged ahead, a more contemporary look has been emerging as a front-runner. The sleek lines of the German-made Poggenpohl cabinetry that her company showcases are a prime example of this style. She said this evolution in kitchen design has been occurring on a global scale. You are just as likely to see the same kinds of designs in Germany, Asia or America. This does not suggest a total uniformity of design. Regionally, some styles still dominate and will probably continue to have an influence. For example, "refined rustic" design, featuring knotty alder and hand-forged hardware, has long been popular in the inter-mountain western United States. It makes sense, in an era of improved communications, global manufacturing and easy travel, that styles and designs can quickly and easily spread from one place to another.

Decorative glass adds some charm to this cabinet door.

The bold lines and broad flat planes of Poggenpohl cabinetry are playfully complemented by the fine detailing of the exposed finger joints on the beech-wood boxes in the cubbies.

INTERVIEW WITH PAUL BECKER OF ARENDAL DESIGN

I spoke with Paul Becker of Arendal Design, who was very generous with his time and expertise. As the owner of a cabinetry business, he had some unique insights that he was willing to share.

Paul said that people are requesting bold and interesting colors when it comes to painted cabinetry, although he noted that white kitchens have always been, and continue to be, immensely popular, probably due to the timeless quality that they impart to a design. He gave me a brief history of what's been popular and noted that in the 1970s and 1980s, golden-oak-colored raised-panel cabinets were the standard. That shifted to clear-coated maple. Then darker, richer finishes on cherry came

▲ Center islands can be used as accent pieces with different colors, styles, etc.

◀ Bringing the upper cabinets all the way down to the countertop is becoming popular.

Furniture-style cabinetry has grown in popularity. Here, a display cabinet that mimics the kitchen cabinets was built into a wall as a stand-alone piece.

to the forefront. In today's cabinetry, he has observed a tendency toward eclectic styles. He doesn't feel there is any one dominant or default species of wood that is used — as in the past. In terms of materials, he is seeing a rise in demand for exotic woods like teak, zebrawood and obeeche in particular, that are usually incorporated in designs featuring flat-panel doors.

Even in the face of today's taste for contemporary design, there is still a demand for detailed elements on traditionally-styled cabinets.

Attention to Detail

HINGES

European-style hinges are the gold standard and are used on most of today's kitchen cabinets. They have two major benefits: First, they are adjustable, which means you can be assured your cabinet doors will hang straight and second, they are hidden when the doors are closed, meaning they don't interfere with the look of your cabinets.

They are applicable to any cabinet you may want. I use them almost exclusively in my own cabinetry business, with the rare exception where the hinges are part of the aesthetic. I once built cabinets for a rustic cabin. The homeowners wanted forged-iron strap hinges that added a lot of character to the design. The finished effect was great, but it was the only time in 10 years that I used hinges other than European hinges.

Several companies produce European hinges and most of them work fine. I use either Blum or Salice hinges because they are the sturdiest that I've found,

and the level of finish is better than some of the knock-off brands, which are often made of thinner, stamped steel rather than heavier castings.

Blum and Salice offer a complete line of products, so I know that I'll be able to get hinges for even the most unusual door configurations, which has at times been critical.

Drawer Slides Are Not Created Equal

One of the most important and practical considerations in choosing cabinetry is the style of the drawer slides. Whether your kitchen will feature three drawers or twenty, quality drawer slides are a pleasure to use and they will ensure a lifetime of proper functionality. Inferior drawer slides will save a bit of money up front but can become misaligned and cause a great deal of frustration on a daily basis.

Here's an overview of what's available:

3/4-EXTENSION DRAWER SLIDES

I call these "semi" undermount because the mechanisms mount to both the bottom and the sides of the drawer, which means the metal components (usually painted white) are visible on the sides of the drawer,. This type of slide is the least expensive, and in my experience, they're the most likely to malfunction. Their ability to open only 3/4 of the depth of the drawer is a hindrance. If you have no other choice due to cost considerations, these slides will work but will offer no more than satisfactory performance.

FULL-EXTENSION BALL-BEARING SLIDES

These slides are often chrome plated. They mount on the sides of the drawers, so they are visually prominent. They offer trouble-free performance at a reasonable price and full-extension capability. I use a lot of these in mid-range projects.

PREMIUM UNDERMOUNT SLIDES

These are the crème de la crème. These concealed drawer slides offer a number of benefits and are manufactured by several companies. They consistently

COMPARING DRAWER SLIDES

	PRICE	PERFORMANCE	EXTENSION	SOFT-CLOSE	AESTHETIC
Economy undermount	$5/pair	good	3/4	no	good
Ball-bearing side mount	$15/pair	good	full	no	OK
Premium undermount	$35/pair	great	full	yes	great

Prices are accurate at the time of printing but are subject to change. However, the comparisons remain the same.

operate smoothly and evenly and most provide a "soft-close" feature that my clients like.

Undermount slides offer a great range of adjustment that allows installers to easily align corresponding drawer fronts more quickly than with other slides. This can make a smoother and less expensive installation. Fine slides of this caliber add $30 to the cost of each drawer, but this usually doesn't add up to enough to be a deal-breaker. Even most of my mid-range clients, once they've seen the difference for themselves, feel that a couple hundred dollars added to the total project cost is money well spent. (I wish I had these slides in my kitchen!)

DRAWER SLIDES MAKE A STATEMENT

Beyond their functional impact in the kitchen, the slides you choose will send a message about the overall quality of your project. Full-extension slides are becoming the standard on everything but low-end projects, so, if you're thinking about the resale value of your home, take heed. Savvy home buyers will almost certainly look at the drawer slides in the kitchen for a clue about the level of quality of the kitchen. If lower-quality slides are used, they may be unimpressed and assume that you've tried to cut corners.

A Word About Dovetailed Drawers

Finely-crafted dovetail joinery on solid-wood drawer boxes is often considered the epitome of high-end kitchens, and for good reasons.

Dovetails make a strong joint that will stand up to decades of use — and they look good too. That said, they come at a price, so you should take a look at some of the other drawer options that are available if money is a factor. I would urge you to avoid particleboard (PB) drawers because I have seen too many of them fail at the joints.

Birch plywood is a great option for drawers because it is a strong and stable material. If jointed properly, it will be the backbone of a durable and attractive drawer system. Joinery methods that I recommend are interlocking rabbet or concealed pocket screws. Both of these create clean, unmarred drawer sides. Drawers that are stapled together may last, but they are never considered a premium product.

Planning Your Hood Fan

There are a few things to think about when deciding how to handle the design and placement of the ventilation system that will accompany your cooktop or range. Looks, noise, performance and price are all factors. This section breaks down some of these issues and showcases a few of the possibilities.

HOOD FANS: NOISE LEVELS VARY

When we redid our kitchen 5 years ago, we put in an inexpensive re-circulating fan. The low setting is extremely quiet — you have to listen carefully to even

▲ When you buy a ventilation kit, they generally appear as an industrial-looking appliance that needs to be dressed up on the exterior or concealed within a cabinet. The homeowners of a 1920's bungalow went all-out with a traditional Craftsman-style kitchen.

▶ Even though this kitchen has a rustic feel, the stainless hood doesn't feel out of place. Because its scale is appropriate to the rest of the space, it creates a nice contrast to the traditional tile backsplash, the rustic look of the cabinets and the earth-tones in the countertop.

know that it is on. 99% of the time, this setting works great. However, about once a year, when we burn something, we switch it to the high setting, which sounds like an airplane taking off. How do I feel about the decision after living with this model? Great. I'd get the same one again. The price was right, it looks good, and it works for us.

HOOD FANS: RECIRCULATING VS. DUCTED

Should you go with a ducted or recirculating fan? The answer to this question might depend on who you ask. If you have the option, a ducted setup is probably the way to go because you can be assured that odors and smoke will be cleared from the cooking area quickly and efficiently. However, if the scale or the specifics of your project make this impractical, you will be fine with a recirculating unit. I've spoken to homeowners who aren't satisfied with their recirculating units, however, so I would recommend making sure that the fan you choose has enough capacity (rated in cubic feet per minute) to do the job.

AESTHETICS: IS IT A PIECE OF SCULPTURE OR AN EYESORE?

The past few years have seen a rise in popularity of the designs that use the hood fan as a focal point of the kitchen, and more manufacturers have introduced designs that promote the idea of the hood fan as almost a piece of sculpture. This can take on a modern or traditional look. While many of my clients

enjoy showcasing an eye-catching fan, others would rather downplay this element and either hide it in the cabinetry or eliminate it altogether. This latter solution is particularly important when dealing with a cooktop that is located on a center island. Placing a big metal venting unit above the island can block one's line of sight and is rather disruptive to the wide, open feel that people are often looking for. In this situation, a downdraft cooktop is a necessity. Check with your local appliance specialists for help in meeting your specific needs as you plan this out.

▼ Many homeowners are choosing to wrap their stove hoods with wood. The variations in style are basically limitless. This is a treatment that is simple and unobtrusive.

▲ This modern hood makes a bold statement and fits in well with a modern aesthetic. The tile backsplash echoes the intense, rectilinear tone set by the shape of the hood.

▶ I'm seeing more of this kind of look: A strongly articulated hearth area as an anchor for the whole kitchen. The concept is executed by employing some of the strategies seen here. Adding detail to the area by making the massing of elements more complex and by increasing the scale of the components. A key to this is the variation of depths of the parts. This creates a feeling of balance and thoughtfulness and serves to pull your eye into and around the space. The effect is a hearth area that is visually dominant and at the same time refined.

INTERVIEW WITH JESSE SPENCER FROM GYGI CULINARY ENVIRONMENTS

I sat down for an in-depth interview with Jesse Spencer, an appliance specialist who works with kitchen projects at all levels of the budgetary spectrum. He provided a great deal of information about what today's homeowners should know as they tackle their own kitchen remodels, and he also gave perspective to the situation concerning the economy and how that is influencing remodelers.

Kitchen Remodeling in Today's Economy

Jesse stated that the challenging economy has certainly impacted the way his clients are acting. He said that the mid-range projects have dried up. In our area, this means projects involving homes valued between $300,000 - 800,000. However, he noted that sales are still strong when it comes to smaller projects and for folks at the high end (meaning, homes valued at $1 million+). He speculates that people with smaller projects (for example $10,000) are finding ways to get them done. People with million dollar homes are likely to be less impacted by fluctuations of the economy. The people in the middle are the ones having a harder time trying to find financing.

He noted that his company has seen a surge in the ratio of remodels to new construction projects — with nearly twice as many remodels as usual during the past year. In his view, the motto of "don't move, improve" definitely seems to apply, .

He sees a couple of factors. Declining housing prices have created diminished levels of home equity for many homeowners, and this can make it tricky to get new mortgages. This makes staying in one place seem like the only option for some people. The other reasons are primarily emotional:

▲ This wall cabinet suggests an affinity with what is often called "unfitted" cabinetry, that is to say, a less formal arrangement of cabinetry as compared to a big, boxy, rectilinear configuration where everything matches and nothing stands out.

◄ Because this corner cabinet was surrounded by appliances on both sides, it wasn't going to be particularly easy to get to (you can see that the stove protrudes 4" past the cabinets), but placing the door on an angle provided the best access possible.

◄ This striking, modern range hood is a bold contrast to the fairly traditional look of this kitchen, but its trim profile and linear feel keep it from seeming out of place.

▼ This homeowner decided to take advantage of the area above the stove to provide a storage and display space for some frequently-used utensils. In addition to being practical, it looks great.

He sees a lot of clients who are happy with their area because of the neighborhoods, schools, parks , etc. (But they do yearn for a better house.) Remodeling for these people makes a great deal of sense. He also deals with a lot of empty-nesters in his profession. He likes working with this group because they generally have decades of experience in the kitchen and they are aware — sometimes painfully so — of what has been missing and what they'd like to incorporate into their new kitchen. With this demographic, Jesse often finds that kitchens are one phase of a larger project which may involve an addition or perhaps a general upgrade to the rest of the home.

Unfortunate Budgetary Compromises
He has observed a nearly-infallible truism throughout his time in the business: The great majority of projects run over budget. He says he's seen it time and time again, whether people are acting as their own contractors or have a full design team. The ramifications of this are predictably uncomfortable, but he brought to my attention one of the consequences of this that I hadn't foreseen — that at least 50% of his clients call him at the stage when they are ready for appliances and ask how they can trim the budget. Because appliances are one of the last items to go into a newly-finished kitchen, they represent one of the few ways

that homeowners can try to save some money. This is understandable, he notes, but it almost always produces an unfortunate level of disappointment — suddenly, the dream kitchen isn't what people had in mind. They are feeling pressured to have to make decisions affecting the size and features of the appliances. For

◄ This simple island appears formal and complex by the amount of detail in the raised-panel construction and by the interesting massing — the side panels extend across the entire depth of the island and the back of the island is recessed to provide leg room.

▼ Microwave drawers provide a good height for removing hot food.

example, instead of a double-oven, maybe a single one will have to do. He recommends planning ahead and committing early on to the appliances that you'll want — perhaps purchasing them ahead of time and storing them in a garage — so you won't be tempted to compromise later on and make decisions you might regret.

Appliance Trends

In terms of finishes, Jesse has observed that stainless steel is still king. (80% of the appliances that he sells are stainless.) He mentioned that Thermador, for example, used to offer more finishes than they currently do because customer demand was for stainless.

However, because it used to be one of the major complaints about stainless steel, manufacturers are offering easier-to-maintain, "fingerprint friendly" finishes.

Jesse has sold a fair number of microwave drawers, but doesn't imagine that they will take over the market anytime soon. There are two reasons for this: One is that they cost around $1,000, which puts them out of reach for many homeowners and second is their size. The drawers have a vertical capacity of around 7", which means they are limited in what they can hold. While this size isn't a problem most of the time, it may be enough of a consideration for some people to cross the microwave drawers off their wish list.

He had terrific things to say about steam ovens, and while he admitted that they are a bit of a luxury item, he noted that many people are incorporating them into kitchens and eliminating the need for a microwave.

I wasn't familiar with the technology, but he told me that steam ovens are appreciated for their ability to do everything a microwave does, only better. Because they introduce moisture into the cooking process, veggies and meats come out juicier, and reheated foods have a better texture and consistency. He speculates that they are likely to remain a fringe item, however, due in large part to their cost, which he put at around $2,400.

Jesse said that cabinet-depth refrigerators have become popular in recent years, especially in remodels where space is limited. And speaking of limited space, he introduced me to a compact double-oven made by GE which allows you to fit a double-oven into a much smaller area. This will be a plus for a lot of people.

Panel-ready appliances have increased in popularity because homeowners are eager to integrate the appliances seamlessly with the cabinetry. Panel-ready appliances are generally less expensive, but that doesn't include the panel, which will need to be custom made, so the cost ends up around the same in the end. The complexity and style of the panel would be important factors.

Some manufacturers are offering separate all-refrigerator and all-freezer units. This has introduced new possibilities in kitchen design. For example, Jesse has designed a number of butler's pantries that house the freezer, as it is accessed much less frequently, and the extra storage in the fridge is greatly appreciated.

Jesse has seen a number of kid-friendly kitchen zones which incorporate refrigerator drawers — some even featuring an ice-maker. He noted that this reflects the trend of making the kitchen accessible to everyone in the family.

Two out of ten people will incorporate a warming drawer in their kitchen, and he says that their versatility is under-appreciated. Bakers will enjoy the low heat setting for proofing breads, and at the high setting (220°), the drawers provide additional capacity which can be used not only for warming or reheating but for cooking side dishes and the like.

No matter what your situation, Jesse feels that the best thing a soon-to-be kitchen remodeler can do is take an hour and meet with an appliance specialist at a dedicated appliance store. He stresses that his type of company is best positioned to help homeowners make educated choices — regardless of their budget. He said many people assume stores such as his only cater to the high-end crowd, but this is far from being the case. His own expertise is incredibly broad and it is geared toward letting people know their options so they can get the most bang for their buck. He insists that great innovations are out there. You simply need to take the time to get educated.

The interface of the cabinetry and the stove is articulated in an interesting way. By adding a corner post and bringing out the countertop accordingly, the stove is, in essence, framed and given more visual weight. This covers up the side of the stove and, if necessary, will make a small stove look larger.

INTERVIEW WITH SETH STRIEFEL

Seth is an architect in Salt Lake City and a veteran remodeler who planned and executed a beautiful kitchen renovation in his 1920's home. In addition, he is designing a new home for himself. No doubt, his experience and thoughtfulness will help him to create another fantastic kitchen.

Seth has some advice about how to avoid some of the common pitfalls that homeowners — and even design professionals — can get into. He said it's easy, in today's media-rich environment, to copy something out of the pages of the latest design magazines, but it's important to go slowly and think about what you'll want in your ideal kitchen.

Something might look great on paper, but your own situation probably offers a lot of possibilities that you might not think of right away. For example, should you install a bank of upper cabinets on a particular wall or could you use that space to install a larger window and bring in more light and obtain a stronger connection with the outdoors? He reminded me that "you are what you know", which I think is a neat way of suggesting that we all make choices based on what we've seen. It follows, if you can expand your knowledge base, that you'll have the chance to make decisions you'll be happiest about. Learn as much as you can about what options are out there in terms of styles, materials, finishes and different ways of problem-solving.

We discussed some of the recent trends that Seth has seen in kitchen design. He pointed out an emphasis on sustainability as being important. Building smaller is one of the best ways to make an impact. He mentioned a number of new materials that he uses in his practice. In terms of panels for millwork and cabinetry, he is a big fan

▲ This kitchen is minimal in every respect: Not only does it shun unnecessary embellishment and clutter — but the layout is simple. Most of the kitchen's storage and workspaces are located on a long run of base cabinets on the west wall.

▼ Proper ventilation is accomplished through the hood that was mounted to the underside of an unobtrusive box (it echoes the shelves) that was firmly secured to the studs in the wall.

▲ Upper cabinets are conspicuously absent. Omitting them from the design not only saved money, but, more importantly, it allowed the homeowner to install a pair of windows which let in more natural light and to forge a closer connection with the outdoors. An open shelf holds commonly used dishware at a convenient height.

of bamboo plywood and Kirei board, and countertop materials such as IceStone, and PaperStone.

Another trend is replacing the center island with a table for dining. It adds a nice informality to the kitchen.

Seth has a keen eye for detail, and he reminded me that it is possible to design projects so that the details contribute not only to the look of your project but to its bottom line.

For example, in his next kitchen, he is planning to use walnut plywood with exposed edges. That means there will be no need to edge-band the plywood (which is a labor-saver) and the crisp, multi-layered look will be a prominent visual element. The walnut plywood is inherently a beautiful material that doesn't need to be dressed up with mouldings or other complex design elements, so he plans to use flat panel doors to show off the grain. This is also great for the budget because flat panel doors are less expensive to make than traditional frame-and-panel doors.

▲ These homeowners have all the workspace they need at standard countertop height (36"), so they chose to lower the final section to visually distinguish that spatial area which has a different function. It serves as a convenient area for the storage and display of their cookbook collection.

▶ On the north wall, a custom unit provides lots of pantry-style storage. It also encases the refrigerator for a neat, built-in look.

INTERVIEW WITH APPLIANCE SPECIALIST TROY HANEY FROM MOUNTAINLAND DESIGN CULINARY & BATH ENVIRONMENTS

For the latest news in appliance design, I spoke with Troy Haney from Mountainland Design. The following observations reflect his experiences in the field.

One of the most noticeable trends in appliance design is a movement away from the commercial-look to an aesthetic that is more refined. The words "softer" and "sleeker" describe the newest appliances. The performance isn't diminished at the high end but the look is less industrial.

In terms of finishes, stainless is still king. Some manufacturers are experimenting and trying to find the next big thing, but stainless seems to work for a lot of people in that it is seen as a neutral and can work in a variety of settings.

There has been a trend to use integrated appliances that are trimmed out to match the rest of the cabinetry. Dishwashers and refrigerated drawers are the most popular items to handle in this way.

In terms of luxury items, warming drawers are one of the most popular at the high end. Troy remarked that people who haven't had them before tend to hesitate, but anyone who has updated a kitchen and has one won't go without it. In other words, they seem to be a bit of an acquired taste, but are appreciated by people who are used to them.

Butler's pantries are more common, especially as home sizes have grown and people are looking for unique ways to use all that square footage. Ice machines are common in butler's pantries, as are under-counter or full-height wine fridges.

Trash compactors seem to be waning in popularity. Although they certainly had their heyday a generation ago, very few kitchen remodels incorporate one now.

Troy also had insight into the way people are organizing their cooking stations. Nearly everyone he works with opts for separate cooktop and wall ovens. He says his clients love the flexibility of being able to place the cooktop wherever they'd like, and this is often on the center island. He feels that center islands are evolving and are becoming command centers for the entire kitchen. The only downside to situating cooktops on an island is deciding how to vent them. A hood fan solves the problem, but not everyone wants that kind of look, so downdraft cooktops with ducted blowers solve the problem.

▲ While still considered a bit of a luxury item, the easy accessibility of the microwave drawer is causing it to grow in popularity. The drawers can be easily incorporated into a standard base cabinet. Three advantages that I can see are: First it fosters independence in kids because they can prepare their own snacks. Second, it provides easy access for wheelchairs. Third, it offers increased safety by eliminating the need to reach up to a potentially awkward height where spills of hot liquids are a danger.

▲ Cooktops come in two basic styles: Drop-ins or slide-ins. Shown here is a slide-in that requires a specially built cabinet.

◄ While I don't have a warming drawer in my home, people who do won't do without them.

26

▲ This island sink is set up as a true command center — it faces out into the room so that a person using it can be fully engaged with the other people in the room. It is set behind a raised bar area, which helps to hide clutter on the countertop when viewed from out in the room.

▲ While stainless steel remains the most popular appliance finish, some manufacturers are offering more options to help you create a custom look.

▲ As the industrial-look has faded from prominence, retro-styled appliances have become popular.

▶ As this kitchen transitions into the formal part of the great room, a change in wood finish and style helps set the tone.

▼ This design illustrates some things that are worth noting: Placing a plate rack in such close proximity to the sink helps make cleanup easier and more efficient. Also, there is no need to elevate the cabinet above the sink more than the adjacent cabinets. A person using the sink still has plenty of room. Finally, the tried-and-true dictate about situating the sink below a window can be disregarded with fine results.

Spotlight on Appliances

Your appliances will make an impact on the functionality and visual appeal of your new kitchen, so it pays to spend some time figuring out exactly what you want and need. And, because few aspects of kitchen design evolve as quickly, you'll want to make sure you're getting current info on what's available. My chief recommendation is to visit a dedicated appliance showroom and not just a big-box home improvement store. Appliance specialists can show you a broader range of choices, for one thing, and their knowledge base will be up-to-date. I think they offer the best chance of helping you find exactly what you're looking for. Even if you end up purchasing appliances elsewhere, your best educational opportunity awaits you at a local appliance dealership.

TURNING UP THE HEAT: COOKTOPS

A lot has changed in the past decade or so. Here's a run-down of some of the options:

Gas Burners:

Offer great control and economical operation.

Electric coil burners:

An old standard that gets the job done. They do take a bit longer to heat up and cool down.

Ceramic glass cooktops:

Easy to clean, and they offer a sleek and simple look.

Magnetic-Induction cooktops:

Use electromagnetic energy to heat the pan while maintaining a cooler cooktop surface.

High-output burners:

A pro-level feature, they allow you to boil large pots of water quickly.

Griddles and grills:

These accessories come in handy when you want to cook breakfast for a crowd or grill dinner without an outdoor grill.

Regardless of the type of cooktop or range that you end up choosing, you'll want to make sure that it is adequately vented. The manufacturer's instructions should clearly indicate the size of hood vent that you'll need, or you can check with a sales associate to be sure.

Ovens have come a long way in the past few years. Traditional thermal ovens relied on gas or electric powered heating elements, but convection ovens have become more and more popular. They incorporate fans to circulate heat, which results in quicker and more even cooking. People commonly report that breads are crustier and roasts are juicier.

If you prefer an old-school aesthetic, you can find more options than ever for retro-styled appliances. What's more, many of them offer high-efficiency technology so you can enjoy the look you want without sacrificing performance.

▲ Electric burner cooktop.

◀ Natural gas cooktop.

COST SAVING TIP

It's easy to spend a fortune on appliances, but there is no need to unless you're committed to a particular look. If you don't fancy yourself a full-blown gourmet, but you'd like stylish appliances, it will pay off to look around and educate yourself about the options. You may find you don't need a stove with enough BTU's to power a space shuttle launch and a basic model will suit you just fine. If so, you'll probably be able to find a good-looking stove that fits into your décor without breaking the bank. Appliances generally make up a big percentage of the price tag of most kitchen remodels, so make sure that what you want and what you spend are in sync. Few of us "need" pro-grade appliances, and many manufacturers — even high-end companies like Viking — offer a wide range of options that are competitive at all price points.

▲ Magnetic induction cooktop.

◀ Griddle.

▼ Indoor grill.

▲ Ceramic cooktop.

SINKS

Most sinks will fit into a standard sink-base cabinet, which typically measures 36"-wide by 24"-deep. Extra-large sinks may require a custom cabinet, so factor this into your budget.

One of my wife's requests, when we redid our kitchen, was that we get a large, single-bowl sink. Since we have and use a dishwasher, having two bowls wasn't particularly helpful for us, and the divider in the middle of the sink makes is tough to soak large pots and pans. We found a nice single-bowl stainless sink and haven't looked back. This kind of decision is about personal preference.

In addition to the configuration of the sink, materials choice is an oft-debated topic. Stainless steel has been a favorite for years now due to its durability and practicality. You can find inexpensive models, or you can spend $1,000 on a high-end model. What's the difference? Three things: Finish, styling and material thickness. The first two are self-explanatory and are basically aesthetic issues. The third is a bit more practical. Generally, thicker steel is considered more desirable because it is less prone to denting, flexing and noise transmission when heavy pots and pans are clanged around in it. The thickness is measured in a number called gauge. Most sinks come in 18-, 20- or 22-gauge steel. A lower number means thicker steel. 18 gauge is sufficient for residential sinks.

Not everybody opts for a steel sink. Cast iron is a classic choice, particularly for the "farmer's-style sinks" that have been popular over the past few years, and many of the solid surface fabricators are offering sinks in materials that match their countertops. It is worth looking around and investigating your options — after all, most people don't replace sinks often, so you'll probably be living with your new one for decades to come.

Placing the faucet near the back corner of the sink, rather than centering it, visually opens up the area.

A drop-in porcelain-covered cast-iron sink is easy to install and will last for decades.

▲ Stainless sinks come in an almost endless number of styles and shapes.

▶ Undermount, solid-surface sinks come in all colors and patterns. After they are installed, there is no seam between the sink and the countertop.

TYPES OF MOULDING AND TRIM

▲ BUN FEET: Round decorative pieces on the bottom corners of base cabinets used to raise the cabinetry and create a furniture-like look.

▲ APPLIQUÉ OR ONLAY (laying on): A detailed carved or etched decorative piece installed on the face of cabinets.

▲ CORBELS: An ornamental bracket that may or may not also be structural. These large, carved pieces often support (or appear to support) island countertops, shelving or hood mantels.

▲ CROWN MOULDING: A long ornamental strip with a modeled profile, crown moulding accents the tops of your cabinets, adding height and elegance.

◄ PLATE RAIL: A decorative shelf with a groove for plates.

▼ DENTIL MOULDING: Moulding with tooth-like, closely spaced rectangular blocks.

▲ BUILT-UP MOULDINGS: Several mouldings can be arranged to create beautiful results.

▲ CORNICE: The uppermost section of moulding along the top of cabinetry; usually refers to moulding that meets the ceiling.

▲ LEGS: Both structural and decorative, they support base cabinets, provide a furniture-like look and can support a countertop overhanging an island.

◄ PEDIMENT: A low-pitched triangular gable that sits atop cabinetry. It may have scrolls, scallops, arches or other detailing along the edges or on its face.

▼ TOE KICK: A recessed strip of plain or sometimes decorated trim that fits-and-finishes the cabinets to the floor.

◄ PLINTH: A square block at the base of a pilaster or turned post.

▼ ROSETTE: A carved or milled circular ornament with a floral look; can also be a square with a circular design in the center.

▲ ROPE MOULDING: Moulding carved or milled to look like twisted rope.

▲ FLUTING: Ornamental vertical, semi-circular grooves routed into a pilaster or column.

▶ SPLIT MOULDING OR SPLIT SPINDLE: In essence, half of a spindle. The flat back and half-round shape makes it easy to apply to a cabinet surface.

▼ EGG AND DART MOULDING: Moulding decorated with alternating oval (egg) and arrow (dart) shapes.

▲ PILASTER: A vertical column that is decorative, not structural. It projects slightly from the cabinet's surface and is typically rectangular.

▲ GALLEY RAIL: A front "retaining wall" made from small spindles and strips of moulding.

▲ VALANCE: A decorative panel installed across an open area, often above a sink, over a window, at the bottom of a base cabinet or at the top of open shelving.

◄ TURNED POSTS: Large vertical pieces with a circular outline; may also be referred to as legs, columns or spindles. These may be structural or decorative.

KITCHEN DESIGN DETAILS

Garbage Disposal Issues

Over the past couple of years, I've talked with a few people who have had varying opinions on whether or not we should install garbage disposals when kitchens are updated. A lot of people find them to be convenient, and since habit shapes many of our purchasing decisions, they aren't likely to be phased out any time soon.

One of my clients told me he had heard that some municipalities are encountering problems in processing their waste water because so many residents were using garbage disposals. Waste water from homes that utilize disposals requires more processing, and this increased utilization of resources may be a real concern, particularly in regions where water is in short supply. I would suggest researching the issue in your locale.

How do I handle this issue? I take an old-fashion approach that I'm convinced can't be beat. I've had 8 of these two-legged disposals for the past five years and they work great. Caring for chickens is fun and easy, and the benefits are egg-cellent. When was the last time one of your appliances provided you with breakfast?

Because this kitchen wasn't large, we didn't want to overwhelm the eye by adding too many fussy details. The design relied on a few carefully chosen materials to create some strong design statements. We broke up the flat-panel door composition by installing a plate rack in a cabinet near the sink and dishwasher.

This kitchen used to feel closed off from the rest of the house, so we removed a non-load-bearing wall, which helped open up the kitchen and connect it to the dining room. By placing a bookcase on the end of the cabinet run and facing it towards the dining area, we helped to further imply a connection between the two rooms. We also improved the flow of the space by wrapping the counter around the wall on the left-hand side. This provided extra space for base cabinets, and it allowed us to punch through the drywall and install an upper cabinet inside the wall (the wall on the other side was a dead space above a stairway leading to the basement).

Wine glass storage is easy to accommodate without taking up valuable cabinet space, and this solution makes a nice design statement. You can purchase hangers in either wood or metal — I made these on the table saw using some scrap cherry.

This kitchen features a wall that is unusually thick — the cavity behind the drywall is nearly 11" deep. It used to be an exterior wall except for an opening right here where there used to be a door opening. We poked a few holes in the drywall to determine the rough size of the opening, then we tore into it with a jigsaw and cut a hole large enough for a cabinet. It holds a recycling bin and makes clever use of an otherwise neglected space.

We could have taken these cabinets all the way to the ceiling, and it would have provided more storage, but there would have been a downside. The additional storage would have been inaccessible for daily use (although it would have been handy for storing infrequently-used items). Also, we would have created a large and imposing mass that might have visually overwhelmed this small room. By keeping the mass smaller and lighter, we showed some sensitivity to the scale of the room, which plays an important role in how people feel when they're in there. If it is too crowded, that can create an uncomfortable setting that would detract from the kitchen as an otherwise fun place to spend time. Keeping the cabinet well below the ceiling also allowed us to show off the crown moulding and the ornate corner blocks that accompany it — these period touches are an important part of the character of the house.

Universal Design

Most kitchens stick to well-known parameters in their layout and design. For example, standard countertop height is 36". But these common rules of thumb aren't considerations for everyone. Universal design is an approach that recognizes this and seeks to design homes that are optimally functional for people with special needs or capacities. It often, but not always, is incorporated in homes that people plan to stay in as they grow older.

Universal design is by nature not a one-size-fits-all process and there are a number of areas that it addresses.

Countertop height: You may wish to install work surfaces at varying heights so some tasks can be performed sitting and others can be performed while standing.

Wheelchair access: Can a wheelchair navigate through the kitchen? Is there a countertop or table with open space below it so that a wheelchair user can comfortably access this space?

Compact work area: Young, able-bodied people may not mind a longer distance between the various zones that make up a work triangle, but others may prefer to have all or most of the features they'll need within a closer range.

User-Friendly appliances: Drawer-style dishwashers may be easier to load and unload than conventional models, and side-by-side refrigerators usually allow food to be placed at a variety of heights, thereby providing better access.

Electrical modifications: If a member of your household were temporarily side-lined with an injury or illness, are the light switches, thermostats and outlets easily accessible?

It is beyond the scope of this book to fully examine all the aspects of universal design. If it appeals to you or someone you know, I recommend checking out the related resources listed in the appendix.

Spotlight on Countertops

What kind of countertops should you get? The good news is that you have more options than ever — the tricky part is navigating through all of those choices and making a decision. I recommend visiting some local countertop fabricators, kitchen showrooms or home centers to find out what is available in your area and to see for yourself what you'll like best. If you're at the stage of picking out an exact color or pattern, you'll definitely want to bring along samples of the other finishes that you'll use in the room (flooring, cabinets, paint colors, etc.) so you can see how they look together.

Cubbies are handy for a million and one things — these are sized to be able to fit mail and other odds and ends that might not even relate directly to cooking. It's another way of acknowledging that meal prep is just one of the functions of today's kitchens.

Natural stone will last forever and has some wonderful patterns.

▲ Solid surface, such as Corian, comes in tons of patterns and colors. Sinks made of this material, when attached to a solid-surface countertop, are seamless.

◄ No two stone tops are alike. It that regard, your stone countertop is the only one of its kind!

02

MAKING IT YOUR OWN

Introduction and Planning: Where Do You Start?

Planning out the look and feel of a new kitchen is daunting to some people, but with the right planning and support, there's no reason it can't be an enjoyable process that yields great results you'll appreciate for years to come. The great thing is that we are lucky enough to live in the information age, so there is no reason to go it alone. By taking the time to research the resources that you have available, you can ensure that you're fully educated about your design options and also have a good idea of what to expect from the construction process.

What kinds of resources can you draw from?
• talk to friends who have remodeled in the past
• visit kitchen showrooms and home centers
• look at books and magazines
• if you're inclined, assemble a file of ideas; magazine and catalog pictures that you like
• work with a professional kitchen designer or interior designer
• books
• the internet: Forums on remodeling, etc.

There are a number of ways to start the planning process. I should point out that it isn't always a perfectly linear journey. Remodeling one of the most complex and important parts of your home requires thinking about the project from a number of different perspectives. You'll probably find yourself pulling ideas from all over the place and ultimately forming a game plan to guide the way.

One of the first questions that I ask people about kitchen design is what kind of scale they see the remodel taking — are we talking about a light aesthetic overhaul, which may be limited to cabinet re-facing, new appliances and new countertops? Or are they adding 500 sq. ft. and getting into big structural work that will require a lot of forethought and outside expertise?

I think of kitchen remodels fitting into a spectrum that ranges from a minor facelift to a major addition. Being aware of the ramifications of each level of the remodel is important. When you're planning your project, you don't want to get into more than you bargained for. Even the most modest of undertakings have a way of escalating and taking more time and money than you initially planned on.

Here is a list of specific questions to ponder as you consider the scale of your project.
• How much do you want to bite off?
• What else is going on in your life?
• Is this a good time for a big project or are you already stressed out?
• What are your goals for the project?
• How will you finance it?
• How long do you plan to live in the home?
• Have you remodeled before? Do you know how the process works?
• Are your expectations in line with your budget?
• Are you going for a high-end kitchen or are you wanting a budget-conscious facelift ?

To help define the various scales that your project might fit into, I've created five categories:

A facelift. It can pay off big time — and most changes are cosmetic. It'll generally take just a few days. Sample budget: $500-$3,000.

A substantial upgrade of the existing layout. Utilities aren't moved, electrical overhauls aren't undertaken. Generally this means new cabinets, countertops and appliances. This will take a week or two, depending on whether or not you're putting in new flooring. Sample budget: $6,000-$15,000.

A new configuration of the existing space is undertaken. This may involve changes to plumbing lines, HVAC system updates, drywall repairs and electrical upgrades. It could take from a couple of weeks to a month. Sample budget: $10,000-$30,000.

Minor structural work. For example, a wall is removed and replaced with a beam, a pass-through is cut out to let in more natural light and connect with an adjacent space, and windows and doors are relocated or enlarged. This could take a few weeks to more than a month. Sample budget: $20,000-$50,000.

Major structural work. For example, an addition. This means big changes — it will be slow and costly. Such a project can easily last 6 months and cost upwards of $100,000.

These categories are not hard and fast divisions, but they help illustrate the varying levels of complexity that homeowners find themselves addressing. It also provides a way to indicate the degree to which you may need to get the pros involved. If you plan to do the work by yourself, and you have enough tools and experience to do the job correctly, you can probably pull off projects in categories 1 and 2 and maybe even category 3. Categories 4 and 5, however, will require some professional expertise in the form of architects, structural engineers and contractors.

Regardless of the scale of your project, you'll want to check with your local building authorities to make sure that you are in compliance with all local building codes and procedures. Be aware that some projects will require a permit, so the idea of being your own contractor may not always pan out. For example, in many areas homeowners are allowed to do their own interior wiring, but not if it involves the electrical panel. So, you may be able to do a fair bit of the work in terms of running wires and the like, but you'll need to call in a pro to hook it all up to the electrical service. Additionally, it may pay to consult with an electrician initially so you can plan appropriately. I'm willing to bet that most homeowners don't really know how many outlets are required and in what locations. Building codes have a number of requirements that are unique to kitchens, and you'll need to know what they are and pay attention to them.

Will you need to get a building permit? Probably. It will depend on what your project entails, and also the specific requirements of the municipality that you live in. Again, be sure to check in with the building department in your area. Some cities have historic district designations that may either limit or closely monitor the aesthetic and material choices that you make, so it is worth looking into this. I once had clients who didn't even know that their neighborhood was designated as historic, and this caused the building inspector to look a bit more critically at their plans and their progress. Many areas have comprehensive information on their websites regarding permitting issues, so the internet is a good place to start if you have questions.

Money-Saving Strategies

This is a good time for me to state the obvious: The scale of your project and your budget needs to be reconciled if you're going to get past the planning stages. It is easy to have champagne tastes and a diet-cola budget, so here are some tips to bear in mind if you're having a hard time aligning your dream with your reality.

MONEY-SAVING TIPS

Be your own contractor

If you have the time and inclination, you might save some money by coordinating the project yourself

Work in phases

Breaking the project down might help with the sticker shock. For example, new cabinets this year, and new appliances next year (or vice versa).

Do less

Scaling back a project's size may be enough to make it work. Working cleverly within the existing floor plan, for example, instead of adding additional square footage.

Do it yourself

I realize that not everyone is handy, but if you're inclined, nearly every project has at least a few elements that are feasible for even the most novice do-it-yourselfer.

Shop for bargains

I have a client who purchased a sink that she won't be installing for a couple of years, but the $500 savings was too much to pass up. If you have time, amassing on-sale components like this can add up in a big way.

Don't touch the wiring

Assuming that your current wiring is safe, you can save a lot by leaving it alone. Even minor modifications like adding a few outlets or a light fixture can

PROJECT MANAGEMENT

To avoid problems during the remodeling process, try to make as many design decisions as possible before the construction gets underway. This isn't always possible, but remaining flexible to unforeseen situations is key. Having your house torn apart is stressful enough without adding to the chaos by needing to pick out tile or backsplash material, for example. Some people are okay with having things up in the air more than others, so be honest about who you are and go with that.

cost more than you think: I have a client who ended up having to upgrade their service panel and this killed their budget. It is worth it to get a free estimate for such work, but keep in mind how much you're willing to bite off if push comes to shove.

Don't make major layout changes

Most big changes to a kitchen layout will require moving plumbing and/or gas lines, and this usually means at least two trips by a qualified plumber.

Chose standard finishes on cabinetry

Custom finishes on woodwork can add a lot to a project's cost. If you consult with your cabinetmaker, you may be able to find a standard finish that you love just as much.

Do it all at once

This may sound counter-intuitive, but you may find that it is more efficient and therefore less expensive to combine a couple of related renovations into one project. For example, if you're updating a kitchen and would also like to remodel a nearby bathroom, your contractor may be able to save you some money by doing both projects at the same time. Think about it. If you need to open up the walls to access plumbing, and then repair them afterwards, it would be a big time saver to do it once rather than twice.

This approach may be more hectic in terms of its impact on your day-to-day lifestyle during the remodel, but then again, maybe it is easier in the long run to just get it all over with at once rather than work in phases. The answers to these questions will depend on both the costs you get from your contractor and considering your living situation.

THE AESTHETIC SIDE OF THINGS

At the same time you're thinking about how large or small of a project you can bite off, you're thinking about specific design ideas, materials, finishes and the look and feel that you're going for. To help with this, I recommend making a folder of design ideas. It should include anything and everything kitchen-related that appeals to you. I encourage people to print photos from the internet, make sketches and clip out ideas from magazines. All of this research and brainstorming will pay off later when you start to communicate with the people that will be involved in your project. The more specifically you can describe your vision, the better.

SPOTLIGHT ON TRENDS:
MATERIAL CHOICES THAT MATTER
  Backsplashes:
- Tile offers more options than ever before in traditional and contemporary styles.
- Whole walls of tile can be installed, it's not just relegated to being installed below wall cabinets anymore.
- Beadboard is a wooden element that can tie in with the cabinets and create a more built-in look.
- Metal pressed tin and the like can help create a vintage look.
- Display and storage options are plentiful. Utensil racks on backsplashes are undeniably convenient.
  Flooring:
- Cork is easy on the feet.
- Bamboo is a sustainable product that suits many contemporary designs.
- Forbo (the original linoleum) is offered in a wide range of colors.
- Tile is a kitchen standard and is easy to clean and extremely durable.
- Hardwood can be sealed perfectly well for day-to-day use in a kitchen.

Putting It All Together

Because any remodeling project is unique to your situation, it will take on a life of its own. You may or may not follow these steps exactly as I've outlined them, and you'll probably find that they may not emerge as distinctly separate phases but may instead overlap and co-exist. Remodeling isn't an exact science and every remodeler is different.

1. Fantasizing, brainstorming and education can take up to 4 weeks. I recommend spending a fair amount of time in this phase. Some people find it is easier for them to visualize a finished product, while others need the assistance of design professionals. Whatever your personal situation, I recommend looking through magazines, visiting kitchen showrooms, surfing the web and generally just mulling over what you'd like in a new kitchen. Make sketches, write wish lists, whatever.

2. Evaluation should take about 1 week. Include budgeting and financing, which can determine the final project's scale and details. Once you have a sense of what you'd like to accomplish, it is time to get a bit more centered and evaluate what is realistic for you.

3. Assembling a team can take a couple of weeks or so. Who else needs to be involved? The answer to this is determined by your project. Depending on your preferences, the scale of your project, and your budget, you may decide to work with the following professionals:
- Architect
- Kitchen designer
- Contractor & various subcontractors
- Cabinetmaker
- Interior designer
- Building inspector

If you are at least moderately skilled and very motivated, you may not need to get anyone else involved.

My favorite way of recruiting design professionals is by referral. A recommendation from someone that I know and trust goes a long way. This will often provide an opportunity to see their work in person (for example, in the recently remodeled home of a friend) as compared to just picking a name out of the yellow pages or online.

4. Final planning takes about 4 weeks. This phase of the process integrates the experience and expertise of the professionals that you're working with and creates a solid plan of action. The financial planning should be distilled from what you can spend into a detailed budget that accounts for everything you'll be doing. Specific decisions are made and priced. In step one, you may have been thinking about expanding the kitchen, adding a set of French doors and putting in top-of-the-line appliances. In step 4, you put a price tag and a time frame with each of these ideas and decide whether or not those numbers work for you. When this is done, you figure out how the logistics will proceed. You may need to come up with viable alternatives and plan from there. You should be compiling documents at this stage, including cabinet layouts, estimates for design services, quotes from appliance dealers, etc. Any changes, updates or misunderstandings about project specifics should be cleared up before physical work starts. If permits will be required, now is the time to get them.

5. Demolition can take one day to 1 week. This phase usually goes quickly. Old cabinetry and countertops, for example, can usually be removed in a morning or so. Taking down walls, can take a little more time, and gutting a room will definitely take a while and make a huge mess. Small things can make a difference, however, such as positioning your dumpster as conveniently as possible on-site to speed up the removal of debris.

Some areas have green dumpsters where debris is sorted for re-use and recycling.

6. Construction/new work takes 1 day to a few months. Depending on the size of your project, there may be very little construction to contend with. Maybe you're simply removing old cabinets and replacing them with new ones. On the other hand, you may spend 3-6 months gutting walls, updating electric and performing structural work or adding an addition.

7. Installation will take a few days to 2 weeks. Once the room is ready; appliances, cabinets, countertops, plumbing fixtures and more can be brought in and installed. This may require some juggling in terms of scheduling the subcontractors. For example, a tile floor can be laid early on, but a backsplash can't be put in until the countertops are set. And plumbing can't be completed until then either. You'll need to have a firm grasp of when each stage of the project will be finishing up so you can plan ahead and start the next phase without too much downtime between. If you're working with a contractor, this is what you're paying them to do.

8. The wind-down starts as the dust settles, you'll realize there are a few loose ends to tend to. As you move into and begin to use your new kitchen, things can become obvious that you would like changed. And note that large projects will have a lot of loose ends that can take a while to fix or resolve.

SHOULD I BE MY OWN CONTRACTOR?
Good question. I am asked this question a lot, and the answer depends on how much experience you have with remodels and how much you really want to. If this is your first time, and the project is a particularly ambitious one, you may be biting off more than you can chew. On the other hand, your personality and your situation in general will influence your decision to a large degree. Some people are, by nature, more inclined to want to act as ringmaster while others aren't. Some people are genuinely curious about how all the moving parts work together, while others are really just interested in having a finished product that meets their expectations. Most people who are thinking about acting as their own contractors are doing so out of either a desire to save money or an earnest desire to be involved with all aspects of the project. If you have a complicated project and you are trying to save money but you aren't truly interested in the nitty-gritty of the project, I advise you to avoid temptation and hire a pro.

Smaller projects don't need a contractor or project manager, per se. If you're just replacing cabinets and countertops, then that is something that nearly any homeowner should be able to coordinate just fine. You'll need to:

1. Plan the new cabinetry and tops and get it scheduled.
2. Hire someone to remove the old stuff or do it yourself.
3. Have the new stuff installed or install it yourself.

If you're not interested or able to do it yourself, you'll need to schedule a plumber to unhook the sink and dishwasher and hook up the new ones.

I had a pair of clients a couple of years ago who followed this plan with great success. They did all of the demolition themselves, and they upheld the practical, environmentally-friendly, and time-honored tradition of installing some of the old cabinets in the garage to enhance its organizational capacity. They laid down a beautiful slate floor during the downtime and tiled some lovely backsplashes once the countertops were in — all of this without the aid of a contractor. The project was kept to a lean budget because they didn't mind getting their hands dirty.

A complex project may have a lot of phases and faces to coordinate — permits, inspections, subcontractor supervision and scheduling. A partial list of subcontractors might include handymen, drywall installers, framers, plumbers, electricians, cabinetmakers, flooring specialists, tile-setters, HVAC installers and countertop fabricators. Just finding people to fill all of these roles could be quite an undertaking. Most good contractors will already have a network that includes these various tradespeople. That is a major benefit of working with a contractor because he or she may be able to offer a convenient "one-stop shopping" kind of experience which will save you a great deal of time, effort and, more than likely, frustration.

THE HANDYMAN
While we're taking a look at the people who might make up your professional team, I've been involved with projects where my clients enlisted a multi-skilled handyman with great results. Although they are not all created equal, they may offer less-expensive rates than a full-service contractor but still be able to provide the kind of expertise that you need for a particular phase of your project. You may recruit them to assist with demolition, to replace a window or two, or perhaps for a great deal of the work. Some of my clients found a very experienced and conscientious handyman who put up sheetrock, installed a tile floor, installed new lighting and more. His prices were quite reasonable and he provided a great level of service and commitment to the project. If you can, I suggest getting a

recommendation and references from a friend or one of the other design professionals that you're working with. Many kitchen designers or cabinetmakers might already know someone who is well-suited for your job.

REMODELING IN A HISTORIC DISTRICT
Our neighborhood is considered a historic district, so this means that even simple projects have to be approved by the building commission. Although this is particularly important when renovations affect the outside of the house, some municipalities will send officials to look for projects already underway and make sure they're going through proper channels. Even interior work can be subject to a lot of requirements. Most licensed contractors will insist on proper permitting, and you may need to factor this into your planning process, particularly as it applies to scheduling. Depending on where you live, this may add a few days or weeks to certain tasks while you wait for inspections or approvals. I recommend talking with your contractor ahead of time so you fully understand how a local planning commission will be involved with your project. It never hurts to call them directly, either.

Demolition can be done by you, or you may want to hire someone to do it. You never know what surprises might be hiding behind those walls!

QUIZ #1: ASSESSING YOUR CURRENT KITCHEN

What are you currently lacking?

_____

_____

What works for you in your present kitchen?

_____

_____

How do your current appliances work for you? Any changes needed there?

_____

_____

Who uses your kitchen?

_____

_____

Does your kitchen work for everyone who uses it? Any special needs or requests?

_____

_____

Do you have enough workspace? Is it at the right height?

_____

_____

How's the lighting? Can you see well at all times? Does the lighting add to the ambiance?

_____

_____

What kind of stuff do you cook? Big elaborate meals or just microwave and sink kinds of stuff?

_____

_____

Is traffic flow manageable? Are people always bumping into each other?
Do three doorways converge in one spot? Is there a way you could remedy this?

_____

_____

QUIZ #2: PLANNING FOR YOUR NEW KITCHEN

How do you imagine your new kitchen being used? Just for meal prep, or as a true social hub?

_____

_____

What do you admire in other kitchens? Of that, what is functional, and what is aesthetic?

_____

_____

What fantasy items have you seen in magazines, showrooms, etc?

_____

_____

How big of a project are you willing to tackle? Able to afford?

_____

_____

Are you trying to enlarge the footprint of the kitchen or simply improve it?

_____

_____

If enlarging, then are there other spaces around the existing kitchen that could be incorporated?

_____

_____

If enlarging the kitchen isn't an option, could you add a window or skylight?

_____

_____

Do you need to relocate doorways to get more wall-space or improve circulation? Can you?

_____

_____

Are you interested in changing the layout of the kitchen or just updating the current layout?

_____

_____

QUIZ #3: WHAT'S IT GOING TO COST?

This worksheet should help you to come up with a budget for your project.

Consultations/Design fees: _____

Permits: _____

Dumpster/Disposal costs: _____

Storage fee:_____

Cabinetry: _____

Trim (for windows, baseboard, etc): _____

Countertops: _____

Windows:_____

Doors: _____

Drywall:_____

Flooring: _____

Electrical: _____

Plumbing: _____

HVAC: _____

Appliances:

    Stove: _____

    Refrigerator: _____

    Dishwasher: _____

    Microwave: _____

Misc. Equipment:

    Faucet: _____

    Sink: _____

    Disposal: _____

    Stove hood: _____

    Lighting: _____

    Backsplashes:_____

Additional Decorative items: _____

Did you need to sit down after you added things up? If the final total surprises you, that's because things can add up quickly. I suggest that you divide this page into three columns so you can see the tally for a budget-oriented job, a middle-of-the-road job and a fantasy-level job. Regardless of what you end up choosing, it is always a good thing to see your options placed in context.

Resale

There are a couple of perspectives to consider when you're weighing the consequences of your remodeling decisions on your home's resale value. Remodeling decisions should be made for your sake, not for the sake of resale value.

This idea will send a chill down the spine of many homeowners, especially those who have made a firm plan to have moved out within a year or two. Those people may do well to ignore this advice, but for anyone who plans to stay in their home for a while, it is often considered wise to make the decisions that suit you without worrying too much about resale value. This approach emphasizes enjoying your home first and foremost, and assumes that in the long run, values do tend to go up in general, so some of the specific choices that you make might feel less consequential when viewed from a broader perspective. It is also reasonable to criticize the annual surveys that attempt to quantify the financial impact of remodeling decisions, because when it comes down to it, it is difficult if not impossible to predict exactly what some future buyer may or may not like. People are individuals and their likes and dislikes can't always be easily categorized.

On the flip side, it is generally considered that kitchen and bathroom remodels will offer some of the best yields when a home is sold, so if you're going to remodel your home, the kitchen is a good place to start.

These questions don't have easy answers. I have a friend who constantly considers remodeling his home but worries that it will be too nice for the neighborhood and that he won't get all of his money back. I remind him that getting 100% back may not be a realistic goal, and besides, what's wrong with having the nicest house in the neighborhood? Furthermore, this perspective assumes that the neighborhood can't change and improve. Frankly, many areas become revitalized because one person sets off a chain reaction when they improve their property, and then others follow suit, little by little. My neighborhood has collectively improved quite nicely over the past ten years, and the home values have risen accordingly — neither of these phenomena would've been predicted by residents twenty years ago, so it goes to show that it just might pay to keep an open mind.

Now, there is one other financial consideration that may factor into your decision on whether and how to remodel, and it is tied indirectly to resale: Comparable properties. It may be the case that you don't feel you'd recoup enough of the cost to make it worthwhile, but if you attempt to sell your home and most of the comparable properties have renovated kitchens and yours doesn't, you may be at a distinct disadvantage, especially in a soft market. When buyer's have a lot options, as they do these days, they're likely to pick the one that is in the best shape, and odds are that they are looking at properties with updated kitchens.

And Now for the Data

Remodeling Magazine 2008-2009 survey of kitchen remodels

MINOR KITCHEN REMODEL

In a functional but dated 200-sq. ft. kitchen with 30 linear feet of cabinetry and countertops, leave cabinet boxes in place but replace fronts with new raised-panel wood doors and drawers, including new hardware. Replace wall oven and cooktop with new energy-efficient models. Replace laminate countertops; install mid-priced sink and faucet. Repaint trim, add wall covering, and remove and replace resilient flooring.

Cost	Resale enhanced	Cost re-couped
$21,246	$16,881	79.5%

MAJOR KITCHEN REMODEL

Update an outmoded 200-sq. ft. kitchen with a functional layout of 30 linear feet of semi-custom wood cabinets, including a 3' × 5' island; laminate countertops and standard double-tub stainless-steel sink with standard single-lever faucet. Include energy-efficient wall oven, cooktop, ventilation system, built-in microwave, dishwasher, garbage disposal and custom lighting. Add new resilient flooring. Finish with painted walls, trim, and ceiling.

Cost	Resale Enhanced	Cost re-couped
$56,611	$43,030	76.0%

This data suggests fairly optimistic returns on your investment, but your personal circumstances will of course be a determining factor. For example, if you plan to sell your home soon, you will certainly take a financial loss, and you'll have to decide how much time you'll need to spend enjoying that new kitchen before you sell so that the loss seems like a reasonable trade-off. For example, if you're planning to move in 5-6 years, well, in the first scenario, you'd be spending about $1,000 a year to have the benefit of the enhanced kitchen. Is it worth it? For me, I think it might be, but that is going to be a personal decision.

The important disclaimer when dealing with the tricky issue of resale is that all decisions regarding the resale value of remodeling projects must be considered in light of trends with the local and regional housing markets. It is well beyond the scope of this book to present in-depth information for every city in the United States. Just be sure to do your homework and talk with local realtors who may be able to help you understand the impact of your remodeling decisions.

For up-to-date information on this subject, as well as a regional breakdown of the data, I suggest you visit: http://www.remodeling.hw.net/2008/costvsvalue/national.aspx

Paying for the New Kitchen

You can enhance the beauty of your home and boost its resale value with a kitchen remodel. However, it's important to choose the right type of financing for your needs. Here are several good options from which to choose:

Mortgage refinancing

If you have a fair bit of equity built up in your home, you can refinance your first mortgage for a higher amount than you currently owe and cash out the difference to pay for the kitchen remodel. It may be possible to keep the same monthly mortgage payment if you extend the time period of the loan. Also, if the project involves making structural changes to your home, the lender may approve a loan based on the estimated value of your home once the kitchen remodel is completed.

Home equity loan

A home equity loan is a second mortgage that allows you to tap into your home's equity. It usually has a higher interest rate than a first mortgage but lower closing costs. And, because the loan is secured against the value of your home, it usually provides a lower interest rate than an unsecured loan. With a home equity loan, you get all of the money that you are borrowing at once, which can be good if your kitchen remodel requires that you pay a large lump sum to a contractor.

Home equity line of credit

A home equity line of credit (HELOC) is a revolving line of credit secured against the value of your home. It is a good option for paying for a kitchen remodel if you need to pay for the project in stages or if you are planning to do the project yourself. You access the money as needed, thus making it easy to pay different contractors or to make purchases at home improvement stores. Most HELOCs have an adjustable interest rate and may provide you with the option of paying only the interest.

Personal loan or line of credit

If you are planning a small kitchen remodel, you may want to consider a personal loan or line of credit. Theses loans typically have lower fees but, because they are not secured against your home, they usually have higher interest rates. Also, whereas the other options are usually tax deductible, a personal loan or line of credit is not.

Once you have decided which type of financing works best for you, contact a lender to get pre-approved for a loan so you will know exactly how much you can afford to spend. And it's wise to tell any contractor you hire that your budget is 10% less than your actual loan amount. Kitchen remodels often have unexpected costs. This will help ensure you have enough money to cover them!

Scheduling Tips

All but the smallest and simplest remodeling projects can be chaotic, and the desire to just "get it over with" is completely normal and understandable. However, a friend of mine is famous for reminding clients that you can have it done quickly, or you can have it done right, and most of the time he's correct.

In my experience, many projects take on a life and schedule of their own as they unfold, and the best thing you can do is to be as flexible as possible and not impose any artificial deadlines on the process. I realize that this advice probably sounds unrealistic, but attitude makes a big difference. I have seen the same old unfortunate situation too many times: People pick a date upon which they hope to be finished, and then they're disappointed and angry when that date comes and goes and the project still isn't done. I don't have any magic answers for making this issue go away, but I encourage my clients to take good care of themselves and do whatever they need to do to keep their spirits up.

Any project's odds of succeeding can usually be correlated with how it is planned out, and I always recommend that people consider the potential impact of scheduling well in advance. For example, the holidays can be stressful enough as it is, but in the remodeling world, this is doubly so. Many homeowners are operating under tight time frames to get projects completed in time for holiday visitors to arrive, and this puts a lot of strain on all involved.

If it is possible, I recommend scheduling your project either well before or after the holidays. Plus, winter weather can have an impact: Icy roads, frozen jobsites, and the like can dramatically slow progress and create unnecessary frustration. If you're working with a contractor, see if they have any advice about when is the best time to schedule your project with them.

Talk about a working vacation

Although this might seem odd to some people, this anecdote proves that creative problem-solving is alive and well, and that it takes all kinds to make the world go around. Last summer, I worked with a lovely young family who were able to coordinate their kitchen remodel so that the bulk of the work (and this included gutting half the room to the studs and running new wiring) happened during their trip to Hawaii so that when they got back, they had much less upheaval to deal with.

They came home tan and rested and their project finished up just a couple of weeks later. This may not work for everyone, but they had done a fine job coordinating the various contractors and making all of their design decisions ahead of time, and it was probably the best solution for them, all things considered. We were still able to be in regular communication via cell phones and email, and seeing digital pictures of the process helped them to know that it was moving along as planned.

The Work Triangle, Diamond and Beyond

In the 1950's building boom that sought to modernize home (and consequently kitchen) design, the work triangle was formalized as a way of planning kitchens. It suggests that the most commonly accessed spots (the refrigerator, the sink and the stove) should all be within a reasonable distance from each other to make meal preparation into the most efficient and enjoyable process possible.

Some rules of thumb for work triangles:
- each leg of the triangle should be between 4' - 9'
- the total of all three legs should be between 12' - 26'
- the triangle should be isolated from household traffic

These suggestions are not set in stone and won't work for every design, but they can be helpful in designing your kitchen.

Fifty years later, the work triangle remains a popular and useful device in laying out kitchens, although some experts have added a fourth station to the equation: The prep area. This common sense strategy doesn't fundamentally change the work triangle as a concept — it just adds to it. The new math might suggest a diamond with a perimeter of between 16' - 30'.

To further complicate matters, you can find references in some kitchen planning resources to multiple work triangles that are laid over each other. While this may accurately describe the way that kitchens can be used in reality, it also might be overkill and cause more confusion than it is worth.

In recent years, many kitchen planners consider the microwave to be a separate area worthy of inclusion in the work diamond. This is a reasonable idea, although it is worth pointing out that all of these concepts are just guidelines, so there is probably no need to redefine kitchens as requiring a "work hexagon". The main goal of thinking about the work triangle is to decide which areas of your kitchen that you see yourself using most frequently and to position them in the most convenient places relative to each other.

Island Design

Center islands have evolved tremendously in just the last few years. They have taken on new shapes, functions and styles as people seek to improve their kitchens' functionality and to express their personal style. Not every kitchen layout will allow for an island, and not every homeowner wants one, but they generally add a lot of character and performance to most any kitchen design.

As center islands have increased in popularity over the years, they have helped to transform some of the most fundamental aspects of kitchen design. For example, the old rule that the sink must be centered below a window no longer applies as rigidly as it once did. Now it is common to see sinks located on center islands so the cook is able to engage more easily with guests. People often situate a cooktop on an island for the same reason. In either case, it certainly points to the way in which cooking is seen as less of a solitary activity and more of a social event.

Islands can be quite simple or amazingly complex in their design. The simplest islands are just rectangular masses with flush countertops, and the more sophisticated might feature work surfaces at varying heights, large overhangs to accommodate seating and unusual shapes to add visual interest. However, even the simplest islands will benefit from thoughtful lighting design. Islands need to be lit appropriately to not only ensure that people can see well enough but to distinguish them as distinct areas. Often you see a row of pendants or a chandelier. Either way, they are visual cues which set the island apart.

In planning a center island, here are a few things you might want to consider:
- Do you want to have seating at the island?
- Would it be beneficial to have a secondary countertop at a raised height?
- What shape would best fit into the room's layout?
- Do you want a simple island or a complex one?
- Do you want to incorporate any display space?
- Are there appliances that would be handy to build-in?
- How will you light the area above the island?

◀ Some islands are being designed to look more and more like furniture. They could have seating on more than one side, which allows adults to have a bit more personal space than being forced to sit side-by-side

▼ Countertop overhangs can be supported by side walls, legs on the corners or corbels.

WORK-SURFACE HEIGHTS

Mixing up the heights of the work surfaces can help to delineate different functions for different spots. In Szykula's kitchen shown below, elevating the bar top makes it clear that it is a hangout spot and not a prep area. This helps guests to feel that they can comfortably relax there without getting in the cook's way.

▲ This island is almost a table. (Distinctive Kitchen Solutions)

◀ The countertop radius overhangs the island, creating a dining area as well as a food prep area. (Diamond Reflections)

▼ Massing an island. In this case, storage, sink, cooktop and open storage.

▲ Display cabinets in an island may be lit to spotlight collectibles. (American Woodmark)

◀ Angled island with nooks and overhangs for one stool here and one stool there. The shape of this island reflects the angles of the cabinetry — or is it the other way around?

Small-Kitchen Planning

Although they can't offer the majestic expansiveness that is expressed by their larger counterparts, small kitchens have the ability to go in the opposite direction. They do the small thing well. Small kitchens will generally cost less than their larger counterparts, but a few small choices may have greater impact. In a large kitchen, design elements may get lost in the shuffle, so small kitchens are all about playing up the visual effect of just a few key design elements. Also, it may be easier to splurge for premium countertops when you don't have that much counter space.

Flooring tile laid on the diagonal will often help a space feel bigger and de-emphasizes any unevenness in the flooring in an older home. My friends Jim and Emily put in a new tile floor in just this way and it worked quite nicely.

If possible, opening up a kitchen to a dining area with just a pass-through to visually connect the spaces and get more natural light in helps the kitchen to feel larger.

At our house, our tiny kitchen feels bigger than it is thanks to 10' ceilings and a window that we cut between the kitchen and our home office. The cabinetry in the home office, which is visible from the kitchen, is made of the same material (cherry with a clear coat). Even though the door style is different, there is a sense of connection between the two rooms, thus making the kitchen feel a skosh larger.

The above approach also allowed us to make use of borrowed space. We removed a door and installed a row of wall cabinets that we use as a pantry for food storage and the like. Everything is still close at hand while cooking, and it cost less than removing the wall between the kitchen and home office. We may eventually get around to that one of these days...

Tucking appliances into other parts of the house (borrowed space) and opening up room in the kitchen footprint can help. It's not always possible but it's worth considering.

Small kitchens do not lend themselves to too many design elements. Keep it simple and use a few key elements to set the tone and feel for the space. Unless you want the cluttered, homey look, don't overwhelm people or yourself by putting too much in a small space.

LAYOUT TIP FOR SMALL KITCHENS

Keeping the space feeling bright and open is a common concern for those of us who don't have a lot of square footage to work with, and common strategies such as knocking out walls, adding windows or skylights and sticking to light-colored furnishings and finishes can all be keys to making it work. I've also found that, when it is practical, eliminating a wall cabinet or two can help a space feel larger. Rather than installing wall cabinets above the sink, where they would take up a lot of room and perhaps feel a bit too imposing, we put in a nice-looking pot rack. This provides accessible storage and adds a bit of visual interest.

Spotlight on Cabinetry

Because the cabinetry makes such a big visual statement, and because it has a big effect on the price tag of the overall project, it is worth learning about the various options that are open to you. One of the major things to know is the difference between framed and frameless cabinetry.

CABINETS: FRAMED VS. FRAMELESS

This distinction used to mean more than I believe it currently does, but maybe that just reflects my perspective as a cabinetmaker who focuses almost exclusively on frameless (also known as European-style) cabinetry. Traditionally, *framed* cabinets were built with a rectilinear frame across the cabinet's front which served to reinforce the assembly and provide a border around the edge of the cabinet that usually showed once the doors were hung. *Frameless* cabinets are just what they sound like: Basically identical boxes without a wooden frame on the front. Since I am an advocate of the latter style, I'll extoll what I see as their benefits.

> *Frameless cabinet pros:*
> Less materials used (more eco-friendly)
> Less expensive (quicker to build)
> Versatile (classical or modern in style)
> Full-overlay looks are possible

The main argument for building framed cabinets is that the frame strengthens the cabinets, but I often find that only to be partly true. Many manufacturers will use weaker ½" or ⅝" thick panels to build the cabinet box and then beef them up with a face frame, but I find this kind of problem-solving to be a bit odd: Yes, the frame certainly lends strength to the box in this case, but personally, I'd rather build a stronger box to begin with. I build cabinet boxes exclusively from ¾" thick panels and have never had issues of strength or stability. The one caveat here is that a framed cabinet may allow you to construct a cabinet with a wider span than a frameless one, although this has never been a significant issue in any kitchen that I've designed. In general, people tend to prefer framed cabinets because they are a more traditional product.

MONEY-SAVING TIP: DON'T BUY INSET DOORS ON CABINETRY

Most cabinets feature what are called partial- or full-overlay doors. This means the doors are hung so they overlap the front edges of the cabinet and can be adjusted on-site to hang evenly. Inset doors don't offer this level of adjustability, so they must be crafted to fit exactly in their openings. This takes a high level of skill and a lot more time.

Although they don't offer any functional advantage, inset doors have become popular these days. Many people appreciate the level of craftsmanship that it takes to create cabinetry with crisp, even gaps between the doors and the cabinets, but you'll see a big difference in the price tag. Is it worth it? You can get quotes for a couple different options and may find that you'll save a bundle by going with overlay doors and still get a look that you're thrilled with.

KNOCKDOWN

Also known as ready-to-assemble (RTA), these cabinets are available at many big-box home stores. They are inexpensive, with the caveat that you'll need to unpack the components and assemble the cabinets on your own. If you're a bit of a do-it-yourselfer and you find a style that suits you, this can be a great way to save some money. Be forewarned, however, that you do get what you pay for. The finished cabinets cannot be expected to be as robust as some of the more expensive varieties, although they will work fine for most applications.

STOCK

This is just what it sounds like. Some of the large cabinet manufacturers offer an introductory line of cabinets that are somewhat limited in features, finishes and door styles, but they can often be purchased with minimal lead times and at reasonable prices.

SEMI-CUSTOM

This term has always seemed a bit nebulous to me, but it refers to a mid-range level of options that is more robust than stock cabinets in terms of finishes, features and sizes, but doesn't have the full-blown anything-is-possible flexibility of custom cabinets.

CUSTOM

The sky is the limit here. Odd sizes, custom finishes and complete flexibility is the hallmark of high-end custom cabinets — and you'll pay for it.

I think it's reasonable to question what these distinctions mean, since they can vary by manufacturer. Rather than focusing entirely on a category, I would advise shoppers to look, first and foremost, for the features they want. This may mean that you need custom cabinets for your application, or it may mean that stock cabinets will work out perfectly. I suggest keeping an open mind and not getting too caught up in labels that seem a bit artificial.

HOW CABINETS ARE PRICED

You will sometimes hear cabinetry referred to as having a price per lineal foot. As a custom cabinetmaker, I have always found this to be a confusing and sometimes troublesome measure. Many manufacturers will quote, for example, $300 per lineal foot for cabinetry. You as a client don't have a lot of information to go on with this. For example, does this include base and wall cabinets? How would a floor-to-ceiling pantry be priced out? Does this include mouldings and trim work? Is installation billed as a separate figure? How about delivery? My goal is to present information in a clear and simple way to my clients and this is what you should expect as you seek out pricing for your cabinetry.

I always quote my clients a total price which includes design time, delivery, installation and everything that is involved in making their cabinetry vision come true. This, to me, is the best way to honestly communicate the cost of the project. If the clients need to trim some money from the budget, then we can break down their options, but generally speaking, the most important thing is to have a dollar amount that is realistic and all-inclusive for your particular project. I often will quote a project in a couple of different ways. For example, a no-holds barred wish-list version and a more down-to-earth, make-some-compromises version. This provides a helpful frame of reference.

THE BOTTOM LINE

How much should you spend on cabinetry? This is a tough question to answer. Even though I am a cabinetmaker, I don't always urge people to go straight to the high-end. I understand that budgeting for a kitchen remodel is a complex process with lots of trade-offs. I recommend that people not compromise on looks. This is, after all, one of the major drivers for the remodel in the first place. If you can find an inexpensive cabinetry solution that looks great, then that is terrific.

I also advise people to make sure that they feel good about the quality of whatever cabinetry they commit to: Is it sturdy, easy to clean, and functional? Are the shelves thick enough to prevent sagging over time? Is the level of finish on par with the other elements of the remodel? I don't want to see anyone spend more than they can afford, but it is also the case that most people only remodel a kitchen once or twice in their lifetime, and I'd hate to see my clients skimp on something that they're going to regret while they live with it every day for the next twenty years.

Layout

This part of the planning is the foundation upon which the rest of the kitchen will be built — what goes

where? All of the lovely aesthetic nuances in the world won't win you over if the sink is in the wrong place. So how do you go about planning the use of space? There are a couple of approaches. As I talked about earlier, the fundamental is the time-tested work triangle.

WHAT'S THE DISTANCE?

However, this is not the only way to lay out a kitchen, and it isn't even practical in every space. Sometimes you're limited by a pre-existing layout, as in a galley kitchen where you don't even have the option of a triangular arrangement, and there are other organizational philosophies to consider. I often advise people to consider the concept of work zones, for example.

SPOTLIGHT ON WORKSPACE

How much counter space do I need? Counter space is often considered the holy grail by people remodeling their kitchens, and with good reason. Adequate workspace will allow more than one person to get involved in food prep, and while there is no guarantee that the family that cooks together stays together, many people enjoy cooking with their kids and spouses. It can be great quality time and a terrific chance to teach valuable skills that can be retained for a lifetime. Inadequate workspace will usually lead to frustration and feeling like someone is always in front of the block of drawers that you need to get into. So, counter space is critical, but how much is enough?

Obviously this is a personal issue and depends on how you use the counters and your personal habits and approaches toward space. While I recognize the need to respect my clients' individual tastes and habits, I usually mention that in many instances, their frustrations about the lack of counter space can be remedied by using the counters differently. In my own home, counters are not landing pads for whatever you're carrying when you walk in the door. I built a large armoire by the front door for this purpose. Also, because the counter space in my home is limited, I don't use them as display areas. I'll find someplace else to put a vase of flowers! The only object that permanently resides on my countertops is the coffee maker, and that is tucked into the back corner where you can't do much work anyway. This may sound like I am a bit obsessive (and yes, I probably am) but the system works for everyone in our home and the lack of clutter helps the space to feel bigger. While my wife and I occasionally find ourselves wanting to stand in the same spot while we cook, we've never in 5 years truly yearned for more workspace. Honestly, if we had more counter space, we'd just clutter it up.

Of course, many people thrive in exactly the opposite environment. They love their stacks of mail, and cherish the 'lived-in' feel of a cluttered kitchen. For these folks, I've seen miles of countertops installed, and they're usually covered up within minutes, to the great satisfaction of their owners. My point is that it pays to be honest with yourself about how you tend to live day to day and plan around that. It is easy to admire the perfectly staged kitchens that adorn magazine covers, but few people have the time, energy or inclination to maintain that level of organization and cleanliness on a daily basis. Thoughtful planning and an honest evaluation of your lifestyle and personal habits can go a long way toward reconciling your fantasy kitchen with your day-to-day lifestyle.

Is the kitchen the first room you enter when coming into the house? If so, it is likely to be a landing pad for stuff. If you're okay with that, then so be it. If it bugs you, consider planning for a cabinet that has the sole function of containing keys, purses, mail, etc. (This also has the lovely side benefit of never having to wonder where your keys are.) If you're lucky enough to have a foyer or mudroom, then it is probably easy enough to integrate such storage options in that space, if you haven't already.

LAYOUT & ORGANIZATION

The *diamond*, basically a next-step articulation of the *triangle*, includes a prep area. Make sure to account for space on at least one side of the stove as a landing pad for pots, pans, etc.

ZONES

Zones are a great way to indulge and engage any special passions or interests that you have or have wanted to have. Baking, or cake decorating, for example. Many a side-business starts in a home kitchen, so having an appropriately appointed one can make or break things in those early days.

BAKING CENTER

A lowered countertop (32") allows you to put more weight and force onto a rolling pin. The mixer could be on a lift-up stand, out of the way of other folks using the kitchen. This zone is self-sufficient except for running water.

FOOD STORAGE

Where do you plan to store your non-perishable food-stuffs? How much space do you need for this? How often do you grocery shop? Do you buy in bulk? Is your storage conveniently located near your primary work area or areas? Do you like the idea of a central floor-to-ceiling pantry?

THE PREP AREA

The prep area should have at least one drawer within arm's length for can openers, potato peelers, etc. Make sure it is not too close to the main sink so that two cooks can work without crowding each other. This area should be near a fridge, pantry or food storage area.

THE MESSAGE CENTER

A message center can be as simple as a whiteboard on the inside of a cabinet door, or as complex as you could imagine. It can include seating (a chair or stool) or be standing height and could have a computer. Phone books, bills, pictures , collectibles, clock, calendar, cubbies, mail slots and files can all be keep here.

COOKING

This zone is divided up now more than ever. While many people (myself included) have a standard-style range which combines an oven and a cooktop, it has become increasingly popular to separate these two functions. The desire to place a cooktop on an island or peninsula where the cook can look out over the room has largely driven this change, in my view. As cooking becomes an increasingly social activity, cooks are less inclined to spend long periods of time with their backs to their friends and families. So, as cooking functions now require more than one appliance, the cooking zone has to be viewed as inclusive of all these things. A microwave is also central for a lot of people.

TABLEWARE STORAGE

Traditionally, silverware is assigned to a drawer adjacent to the sink, and china goes in an upper cabinet in close proximity. This is hard to argue with because it makes it easy to put dishes away when they've just been washed, but I've seen other arrangements that work out well, too.

I have clients who entertain guests on a near-weekly basis, and also need convenience in their daily routines, so they've come up with a solution that works well for them. They store their good china in the butler's pantry that is located in the hallway between the dining room and the kitchen, and their everyday dishes are housed in a cabinet that is adjacent to the sink. The theory is that day-to-day cleanup is quick and easy, but less-frequently used items can be stored a little farther away without imposing too much of a burden.

I also have more and more clients who are storing tableware in drawers located in base cabinets adjacent to the dishwasher. This is simply because it makes unloading the dishwasher that much easier. Many of my clients are empty-nesters who are starting to think ahead about living in their homes during their senior years, and the idea of lifting heavy stacks of plates up into an upper cabinet might seem less appealing in ten or twenty years. Hence the increasing popularity of sturdy base cabinet drawers that are used for china storage.

CLEANUP

This zone is pretty straightforward. For most people it includes a sink, a dishwasher, and storage space for sponges, scrubbers, dish soap and the like. Some people like to use tilt-out trays located below the sink to store these small items, and my wife and I enjoy the soap dispenser that is built in to our countertop — no need to have a bottle of dish liquid cluttering up the countertop. Traditionally, double-bowl sinks have been popular for washing dishes, but as dishwashers become ubiquitous, I've seen people (myself included) opt for single-bowl sinks.

WINE STORAGE/BAR

These areas won't appeal to everyone, but under-counter wine fridges are becoming popular, and some people enjoy taking things to a greater extreme and incorporating full-on bar areas with all the fixings.

Floor Plans

Unless you're building a new home, or are planning to undertake a substantial remodel and have lots of space to work with, your layout may be largely determined by the existing shape of your kitchen. For example, someone with a small galley-style kitchen probably won't be able to create a G-shaped configuration without removing some walls or adding on some square footage. And all layouts need to create not just a functional kitchen, but a kitchen that is optimally integrated into the rest of the house. In my own kitchen (illustrations facing page), three doorways leading to other rooms converge to create a highly trafficked spot. Any remodeling that I might hope to undertake needs to make sure it allows plenty of space for circulation, and

this will affect my other options for laying out the cabinets, appliances and countertops. My wife and I pondered a number of different ideas, including knocking out the load-bearing wall between the kitchen and the office, and replacing it with a beam and a couple of posts on either end. We ultimately decided that we liked having a separate kitchen and office, and that having a larger kitchen wasn't worth losing the office entirely. We could've handled the expense, since I'd be able to do most of the work myself, but after five years, we're satisfied with our decision: For us, having a number of smaller rooms that function as separate spaces works better than having a "great room" kind of layout. But that's hardly an empirical prescription: Personal preference always wins the day.

Our choice to keep the fundamental structure intact, meaning that we didn't alter any circulation routes or move walls, meant that we needed to adhere to an L-shaped layout. If the room had been wider, we could have considered a U-shaped layout, but we didn't want to cramp the small space further by adding another leg of cabinetry. And even if we had the space, doing so would have come at the cost of creating another inside corner as far as cabinetry is concerned, and inside corners don't offer as many possibilities as long runs do.

This gets into an important topic in cabinetry layout: Accessing the space inside a corner cabinet. The subject merits its own section, which you'll find in this chapter, but for the moment I'll simply say that I am not a big fan of inside corners in cabinet layout (this refers to the point where two runs of cabinetry intersect). The chief objection here is that it can be tough to access the stuff you have stored in this area, and it is often difficult or impossible to reach the farthest recesses of the cabinet. So, in my view, adding another run of cabinetry would create an inside corner cabinet, which I personally tend to view as an inconvenient liability, so the new run would have to be fairly long to offset the disadvantage that it introduced. But then again, some people simply want or need more cabinet space badly enough and an inside corner may be a perfectly acceptable part of their overall storage solution!

However, it is worth noting that this analysis looks at the amount and accessibility of cabinet space; equally important in a balanced perspective is the importance of workspace. A U-shaped layout would provide more counter space, and I'll admit that would be nice to have, as both my wife and I often cook together most nights of the week. In our tiny kitchen, it's a moot point, but I would be remiss if I didn't at least address the importance of having adequate workspace.

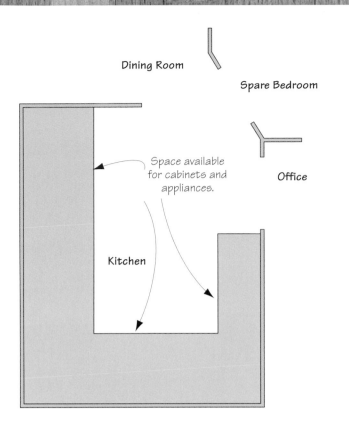

Dining Room

Spare Bedroom

Office

Space available for cabinets and appliances.

Kitchen

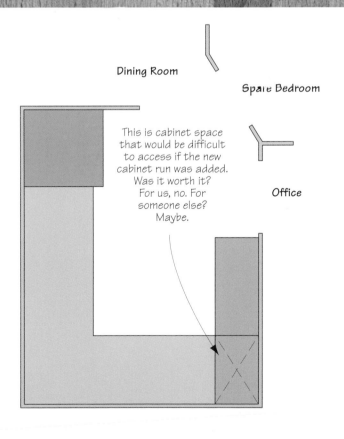

Dining Room

Spare Bedroom

Office

This is cabinet space that would be difficult to access if the new cabinet run was added. Was it worth it? For us, no. For someone else? Maybe.

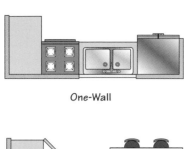

One-Wall

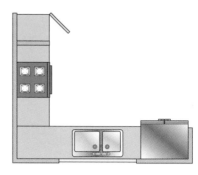

L-Shape

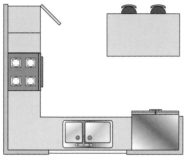

Galley

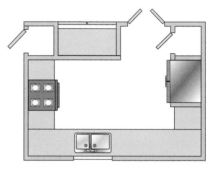

L-Shape with Island

This illustration shows some basic floor plan styles. Most kitchens fall into one of these categories.

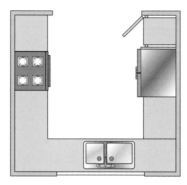

U-Shape

G-Shape

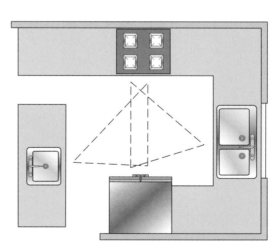

Two-cook Kitchen

This two-cook kitchen doesn't have a center island but it provides plenty of open floor space so people can stay out of each other's way.

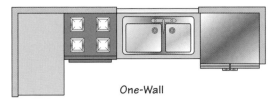

One-Wall

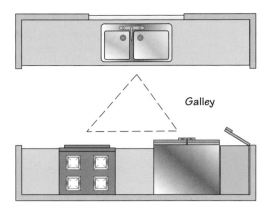

Galley

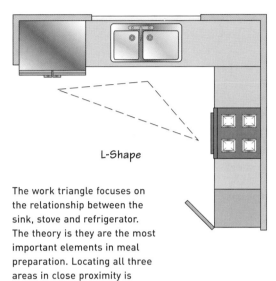

L-Shape

The work triangle focuses on the relationship between the sink, stove and refrigerator. The theory is they are the most important elements in meal preparation. Locating all three areas in close proximity is considered a good and efficient kitchen design.

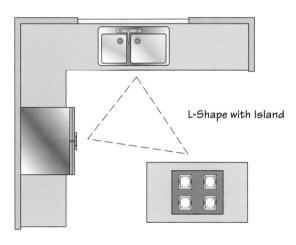

L-Shape with Island

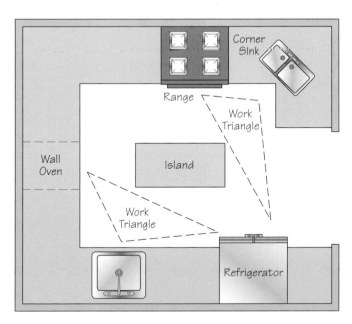

Corner Sink

Range

Work Triangle

Wall Oven

Island

Work Triangle

Refrigerator

U-Shape

In homes where two people cook at the same time, it's not uncommon to think of the kitchen as having two work triangles. This often involves a large sink for dish clean-up and a smaller sink for meal prep. In this case, the island could serve as a work area for both people.

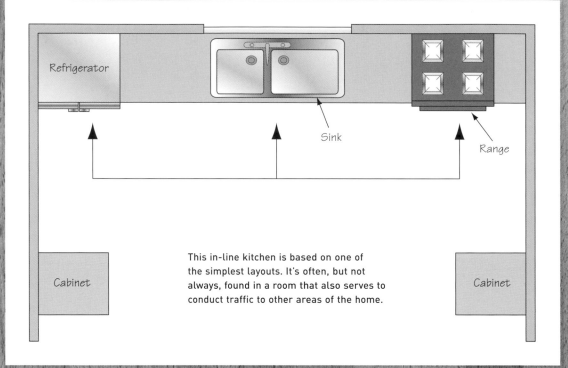

This in-line kitchen is based on one of the simplest layouts. It's often, but not always, found in a room that also serves to conduct traffic to other areas of the home.

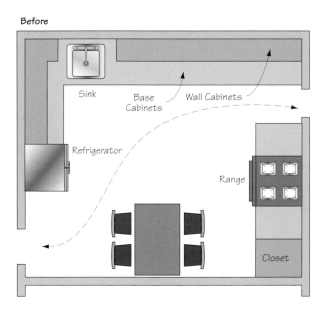

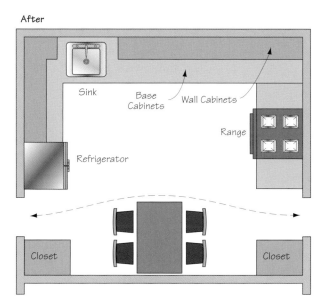

Optimal layouts provide not only an efficient place for a cook to work but also the best possible traffic flow for other members of the household. Ideally, the main working area of a kitchen is sequestered off to one side so that a cook isn't interrupted by people who need to pass by on their way somewhere else. This can often be accomplished by moving a doorway or a bank of cabinets.

Basic Kitchen Specifications

While all kitchens are unique, it helps to have a few rules of thumb in mind to simplify the planning process. The following guidelines may prove useful.

IN-LINE SEATING

If you're designing a center island, peninsula, or any other area that will offer side-by-side seating, you'll want to allow at least 21"-25" for each diner to avoid over-crowding. A children's area may provide slightly less space, but as they grow, an under-sized area could turn into an inconvenience.

CIRCULATION

How much space do you need for traffic flow in a kitchen? Here's a few rules of thumb:
- 36"-42" between cabinetry runs or cabinetry and an island, 48" in multiple cook kitchens
- 32" of clearance behind a table or peninsula for chair clearance, 65" if there is traffic

COUNTERTOP HEIGHTS

- 36" is standard height for work surfaces
- 42" is bar height
- 30"-32" is sometimes used for rolling out pastry or as a cutting/prep surface. These heights can be varied to fit individual preferences.

CABINET DEPTHS

Standard base cabinets are about 24" deep, although this might vary slightly by manufacturer. Custom cabinets can usually be ordered in 15", 16", or 18" depths to accommodate unusual configurations. Standard wall cabinets are 12" deep.

WALL CABINET CLEARANCE

It's usually 18" from the top of the countertop to the bottoms of the wall cabinets. Bear in mind this means 18" of clear space. If you have a light rail attached below the cabinets to conceal under-cabinet lighting, the 18" would be to the bottom of the light rail, not the cabinet.

Kid-Friendly Kitchen Design

As kitchens evolve to play a greater role in people's lives as a place to spend time, it is only natural that some folks have looked at what can be done to enhance the functionality of the kitchen for kids, too. There are a couple of guiding ideas here:

1. Make the space functionally useful for kids so they can be more independent.
2. Make the space appealing for kids to hang out in so the kitchen functions as a "family room".
3. Create storage solutions that are easy for kids to use to help keep the house tidy and organized.

KID-FRIENDLY DESIGN ELEMENTS

A hang-out area, which may feature a pull-out drawer with a desk, or a cushioned reading nook with storage options at kid height. The storage solutions should be simple to use — open a door and hide the clutter.

It can be handy if there is kid-friendly storage near the door. The classic example is cubbies in a mudroom, but a lot of homes don't have separate mudrooms. The most frequently-used entry door often leads directly into the kitchen, so even though allotting cabinet spaces for boots and backpacks might not seem like a kitchen-related task, it may be of real convenience.

Some people build-in refrigerated drawers to hold snacks and drinks.

Refrigerated drawers are a great way to store commonly used items like fresh fruit and vegetables. Kids can access them easily.

Corner-Cabinet Layout

Every kitchen layout style, except the galley, will probably involve the intersection of two or more runs of cabinetry. This means that cabinets will meet at an inside corner. This creates an issue that is worth thinking about: How do you best utilize and access the cabinet space at this junction?

There are a few basic types of solutions for cabinetry in corners:

- Corner cabinets, which sometimes but don't always feature a lazy Susan
- Blind runs, which consist of a rectangular cabinet overlapped by another cabinet
- Inserts which allow specially-shaped drawers to extend into the corner
- The corner sink

Corner cabinets can be designed to angle across their fronts or they can be built with a right-angle configuration that usually requires two doors that are joined together in such a way that they open as one. Both options will work just fine. The major consideration here might be an aesthetic one — do you want your countertops to jut out into the room to follow the 45° angle of the cabinet face or not? There's no wrong answer here, but it is something to consider. Some people like the extra depth and fill the counter space with a microwave or the like, while others feel that this layout eats up too much floor space in the room.

The major issue when two cabinets meet at an inside corner of a room is accessing the cabinet space. It's often a highly contested issue, and most cabinetmakers and kitchen designers concede there is no ideal solution. Every option has pros and cons, so it generally comes down to choosing the option that bothers you the least. In this section, I'll explore this issue in detail so you can make up your own mind.

Corner cabinets outfitted with lazy Susans are a traditional solution to the how-to-handle-the-corner dilemma, but it must be acknowledged that they aren't without their faults. For example, it isn't uncommon for objects to fall off the rotating shelves and wind up in "no man's land" (in the back of cabinet) where they'll never be seen again. It's also true that lazy Susans consist of a circle set into a rectilinear space, and this doesn't use every bit of the space available. For these reasons, lazy Susans have to be seen as a compromise, but they offer fairly good access to whatever you're storing. It is worth mentioning that right-angle corner cabinets can also be outfitted with lazy Susans that attach directly to the cabinet doors — the doors then disappear inside the cabinet as you rotate the mechanism. However, this option only works with inset cabinet doors. See the illustrations on page 65.

An alternative to the lazy Susan is the segmented super Susan (see photo bottom left page 66), available through Diamond Cabinets. It provides a decent combination of efficient storage and easy access, but the trade-off this time is cost. This may or may not be worth it for you, but it is nice to have options.

Another solution, the blind run, is one that I often suggest because of its inherent simplicity. A rectangular cabinet is placed against the first wall. It is partially overlapped by the cabinet on the adjacent wall. This setup allows you to use every square inch of the storage space, although accessing the back corner is admittedly a bit trickier. It is a money-saving option, too, because in addition to being a simpler and less time-consuming design to construct, you won't have to pay extra for a lazy Susan mechanism. And given that even a bargain-basement white-plastic lazy Susan will run you $50, this isn't insignificant.

Corner drawers are a fairly new option, and some people absolutely love them. They provide great access to the contents, but the drawback is increased cost and also a fairly inefficient use of the available space. The cabinets and the drawers are labor-intensive to build. If you have a lot of storage space to begin with, you may not miss the wasted space on the sides of the drawers, but this kind of thing is certainly going to boil down to individual preferences, layouts and budgets.

Some people solve the corner question by placing a sink in the corner. This makes sense from the point of view that the space below the sink is already rendered less usable due to the presence of the plumbing, so placing a sink in the corner cabinet — a tough area to access day-to-day — may be a reasonable fit. It basically frees up the area where the sink otherwise would have been so that it can be outfitted more efficiently. While I can't argue with this, I have personally never been attracted to this type of design. Maybe that is because I have seen too many westerns and prefer to face out into a room whenever possible. The likelihood of being shot in the back by a masked outlaw is probably slim, but this layout really doesn't seem social enough to me. I cook a lot, and I want to interact with the other people in the room and not be made to feel as if I'm being punished and have to stand in a corner all by my lonesome. But that's just me.

WALL CABINET LAYOUT ON INTERIOR CORNERS
The intersection of two cabinets in the corner is a simple matter when it comes to wall cabinets. This is because the cabinets are much shallower here, often 12" deep instead of 24", and this means that accessing the back corner of the space is much easier, regardless of the configuration. You have three choices here: A

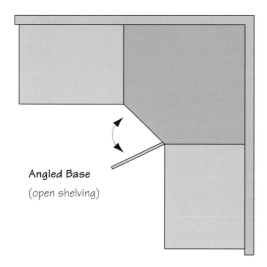

Angled Base

(open shelving)

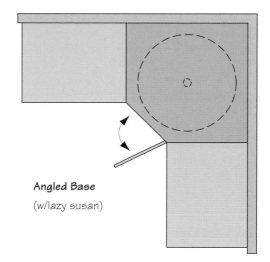

Angled Base

(w/lazy susan)

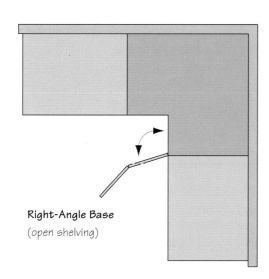

Right-Angle Base

(open shelving)

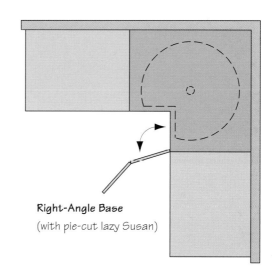

Right-Angle Base

(with pie-cut lazy Susan)

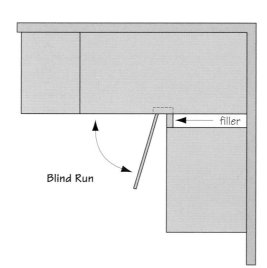

← filler

Blind Run

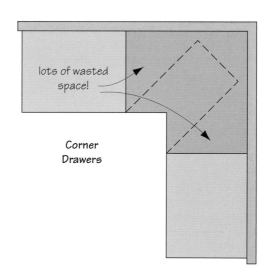

lots of wasted space!

Corner Drawers

corner cabinet, a built run or you can deaden the corner entirely.

If you go with a corner cabinet, you'll gain the ability to access the back of the cabinet from either side. It is often the case that the two doors on this cabinet are hinged at the middle of the cabinet (the corner), because this provides the most convenient way to reach into the cabinet. In other words, the doors, if hinged at the outside edge of the cabinet, would have to be swung out into your face, and you would have to reach around the cabinet door, which most people find rather awkward. I have built plenty of corner cabinets and find them to be an elegant solution. Their only drawbacks are that they take longer to build and they require a less efficient utilization of materials due to their odd shape. Both of these factors add to the cost of the finished cabinet, but it is usually worth it if you're inclined to this layout.

I also build a lot of blind runs because they are quicker and simpler to build (thus more cost effective for the client) and they function quite well. Building them also involves a more efficient use of materials. The trade-off is access: Reaching items stored in the back of the cabinet is a bit trickier, so I recommend storing infrequently used items there. Corner cabinets can provide slightly better access to the back corner of the cabinet, so if there is limited storage, optimizing access to every last bit of the cabinet space might seem more important. Again, these types of choices end up being matters of personal preference.

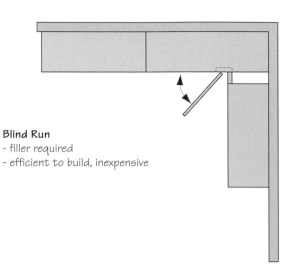

Blind Run
- filler required
- efficient to build, inexpensive

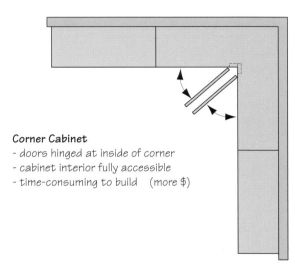

Corner Cabinet
- doors hinged at inside of corner
- cabinet interior fully accessible
- time-consuming to build   (more $)

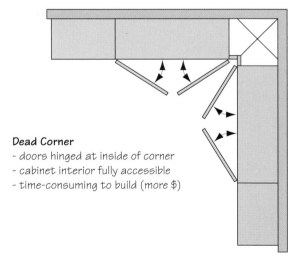

Dead Corner
- doors hinged at inside of corner
- cabinet interior fully accessible
- time-consuming to build (more $)

Diamond Kitchen's super lazy Susan.

ADDITIONAL CONSIDERATIONS
FOR CORNER CABINETS

One of the easiest mistakes to make when making cabinets that meet in corners is to not make the fillers large enough for the doors or drawers to open. In the case of drawers, the filler on the cabinet needs to be large enough so the drawer will clear not only the mating cabinet's door and/or drawer faces, but that the drawers will clear the pulls and/or handles. Nothing is more upsetting than to discover this error at installation time! (A good reason to assemble the entire run of cabinets in the shop before installing them.)

You'll also need to make sure that the doors for the corner cabinet are large enough to provide good access to the cabinet's interior.

Here's a situation where a filler was needed to fill the gap between the cabinets in a corner where there were "two corners". This filler also allows room for the door on the smaller cabinet to be opened. Note that the filler on the larger cabinet is extended past the face of the door on the smaller cabinet by about 3". This allows room for the door on the larger cabinet to be opened.

Getting It On Paper

Having great ideas only goes so far if you can't communicate them effectively to the people you'll be working with, and drawings are a critical tool in the design process. This doesn't mean that you need to turn into Frank Lloyd Wright and create masterpiece renderings worthy of being framed for the ages, but being able to hand a quick sketch to your collaborators early on in the process will help everyone to get on the same page that much quicker.

There are two kinds of drawings that you might want to think about making — the thumbnail sketch and the scale drawing. Again, neither one needs to be of museum quality, but they can both be tremendously useful for a couple of unique reasons. The thumbnail sketch shows the essence of what you're trying to do. You don't have to worry about getting the dimensions exactly right — you're showing the overall way that the components of the design are laid out. You don't need to worry about precision at this stage. I consider this drawing to be a sort of rough draft, and I expect that it will undergo some revisions.

A scale drawing takes the basic concepts presented by the thumbnail sketch and tries to examine them a bit more closely by introducing dimensions and proportions. For example, the thumbnail sketch may describe a particular layout, but once you see it drawn to scale, you may realize that particular cabinet sizes don't look proportional, or that a given wall can't hold as many cabinets as you had hoped, or that the actual position of the window won't allow the refrigerator to go where you had assumed it could.

These kinds of realizations are great because they allow you to proceed in your planning with your eyes wide open and maybe even entertain some new kinds of solutions — could the window be moved, for example, or could its dimensions be changed? Regardless of the ultimate conclusions that you might make, I recommend using graph paper as a handy way to draw to scale. The boxes are commonly used to represent 3" or 12" dimensions, depending on the size of the drawing you're working with.

And since we're living in the information age, it stands to reason that you're not limited to paper and pencil drawings. For $50 or less, you can purchase entry-level software that is surprisingly sophisticated. Even entry level software packages will allow you to create 3D renderings that you can rotate and examine from all angles. The one I use (*Home Design Pro* by *Punch, Inc.*) features a neat "walk-through" mode that allows you to move around the kitchen as if you were actually there. And as the name implies, it isn't limited to kitchens. I've used this software to draw entire houses. This might come in handy if your remodel involves an addition or encompasses adjacent spaces like a great room. The Punch interface is intuitive, so much so that I was able to have it figured out in just a few hours, and I'm no computer genius. If you're so inclined and you are reasonably computer savvy, you'll probably find that the learning curve is worth dealing with because the results can be great. Now that I am fairly proficient with the software, I can draw kitchens to scale and put in all of the cabinets, doors, windows, etc. in about half an hour. The basic process requires you to input the dimensions of the room — which I take directly from my scale drawing on graph paper — and place cabinets, appliances, windows, doors, etc. where you like. The program then automatically generates the 3D models and elevations.

The software is also handy because you can save multiple files and update them so you have alternative designs based on one original set of dimensions. This could be invaluable if you're trying to decide between a couple of different layouts. It is also a lot easier to edit things on the software than it is to redo entire drawings.

Three distinct advantages to using software as a design tool:
1. Helps you to experience what your result will be.
2. Allows you to troubleshoot problems in virtual reality first.
3. Provides drawings for your use and for anyone else who is involved (spouses, contractors, etc.).

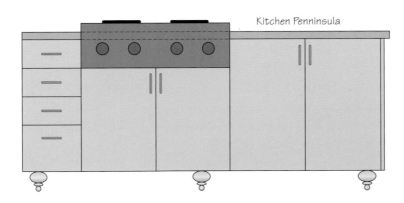

Kitchen Penninsula

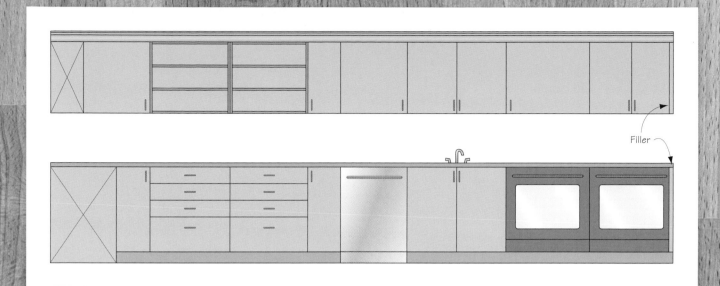

Filler

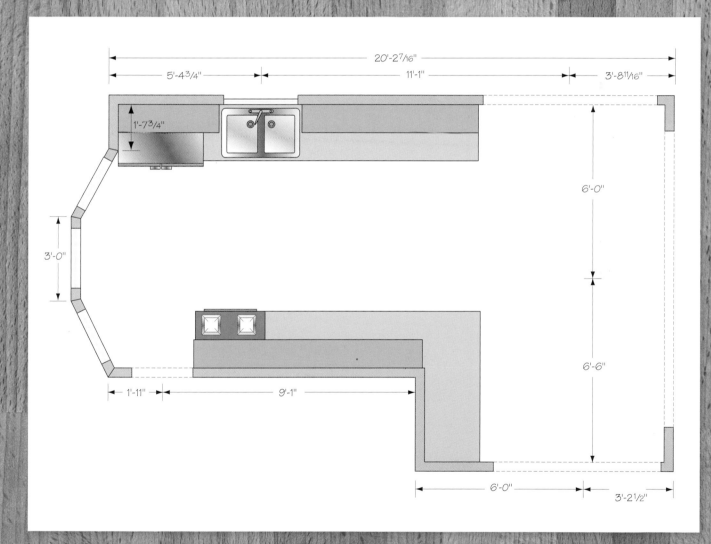

03

DO IT YOURSELF

In the interest of full disclosure, I admit that I am a die-hard do-it-yourselfer (DIY). Many of the projects that I've tackled in my own home never would have happened if I had to pay professionals to do the work, so I see the exchange of sweat equity as a bargain. It is also the case that I'm lucky to have the tools and resources of a full-time woodworker, so I recognize that not everyone may be as prepared as I am. I also recognize that not everyone has the inclination to roll up their sleeves and work on their homes, and that all of us have a limit to what we can do.

Even I had to finally call in an electrician recently when the task was beyond my abilities. Being honest with yourself about your skill sets and your general level of preparedness is critical for anyone considering a DIY project, and *knowing when to call in the pros is essential*. The stakes can be high in remodeling, and I'm not just talking about the stress that it can impose on a marriage: Some projects can be physically dangerous, so be careful.

Now, if you're still with me, great. I've included a couple of DIY projects that I think you might enjoy. If you're an experienced woodworker, you'll find a detailed tutorial on building your own cabinets. Not only will you save a fortune, but it is a tremendously satisfying process that may be easier than you think. I've also included information on installing cabinets, which can also save you thousands of dollars. And on a simpler scale, I documented the layout and installation of a glass mosaic tile backsplash — something that nearly anyone can do in an afternoon with only a couple of tools required.

Even if you have no interest in performing these tasks yourself, you may find it interesting to see how they come together. Simply knowing the process is a valuable resource.

A DIY Remodeling Success Story

Mike and Elisha are truly an inspiration to everyone who has considered tackling ambitious projects on their own. Mike works full-time for himself as a designer and concrete fabricator, so he is no stranger to kitchen remodels, but it is worth pointing out that before undertaking his own kitchen, he didn't have any experience building cabinets or executing projects on this scale. I think he exemplifies what is possible, however, if you have a few tools, a vision, and the patience to see it through.

Mike laughs now when he states that the house was a dump when they bought it. He maintains that they purchased it not because of what it was, but because of what they knew it could become. Their vision paid off in spades. By doing the lion's share of the work themselves and by being patient with the process, he and Elisha were able to totally remodel their kitchen into a gorgeous, highly functional space, and they did this for under $5,000.

When they moved in, the entire main floor of the house needed an upgrade, and the kitchen came as the final phase of the whole project. This allowed Mike and Elisha to live in the home for nearly a year and really get a feel for what worked and, more importantly, what didn't work about the kitchen as it was initially configured. Their main complaints prior to the remodel were that the kitchen layout wasn't optimal due to an awkward circulation pattern, and that the rooms didn't have a particularly bright, open feeling.

They remedied this by tackling some structural work at the beginning of the kitchen project.

The modern feel of the kitchen is echoed in all the details. For example, integrating the outlets into the backsplashes creates a sleek look. But there is more going on here than meets the eye: The back wall is solid brick, so by designing backsplashes that were thick enough to conceal a shallow outlet box, Mike avoiding the hassle of having to cut into the brick.

Specifically, this entailed covering up a door on the west wall so that they could use that wall to create a more useful cabinet layout- including room for a modern-sized fridge, which was never accounted for 80 years ago when the house was built. They also opened up a breakfast nook at the back of the kitchen to gain some helpful storage and seating space, and most importantly, to let the light flood into the rest of the home. They continued this trend of opening up the space by enlarging the small doorway at the front of the kitchen to help connect the kitchen to the dining room. Mike is pleased with the result, and noted that opening up walls and helping light to flow better can make a dramatic difference in helping a small home to feel bigger and more comfortable.

Mike and Elisha greatly appreciated the addition of a dishwasher, which took up some space that was formerly used as storage, but fortunately they added on a lot of cabinetry compared to the original configuration, so they came out ahead in terms of storage capacity.

Because this beautiful project was accomplished on a very modest budget, Mike found lots of ways to cut costs without cutting corners. For example, he visited used appliance dealers in their city and found great deals on models in immaculate condition that were only a year or two old. They saved over 50% compared to the cost of brand new ones — with no downside.

After the structural work had been initiated, Elisha got her electrician brother involved to help out with a much-needed update to the electrical system. As this critical aspect of the project got underway, they planned out the overall layout of the kitchen, and Mike headed to his workshop to build some cabinets. The couple was sold on the idea of using light-colored bamboo for the cabinet door and drawer fronts, and even though it is an expensive material, they didn't really need that much of it, so the overall cost was still quite reasonable.

As the project progressed, the various elements all fell into place. Mike recalls that he found the faucet on sale for only $50 fairly early on, and by taking things a step at a time, they were able to pull-off the facelift without too much overall disruption. Coordinating the various phases of the project required some planning, to be sure, as it took about 5 people to lift the heavy concrete countertops into place, but it was well worth it. Mike said they were without a kitchen sink for about a day. It didn't happen overnight, but the results speak for themselves. Mike and Elisha have clearly demonstrated that it is possible to pull off a top-notch project on a small budget if you can do some or all of the work yourself, and if you can be flexible and creative along the way.

◄ Undermount sinks are often paired with concrete countertops — it's a great way to showcase the beefiness of the countertop, and it makes the sink/countertop interface easier to clean than a drop-in sink as there is no place for grime to accumulate. Mike chose a medium-sized single-bowl sink that looks great with the iconic faucet that he picked up for just $50.

▲ The base cabinet that Mike built is a terrific example of what can be done for very little money if you have a few tools at your disposal. Mike and Elisha bought the wine rack for $10 and then Mike built the cabinet out of scraps. A custom cabinet like this would easily cost $500.

◄ Mike is a professional designer and concrete fabricator. He created this sculptural element as an understated focal point in the breakfast nook. The cast-in bowl on top could also be used to hold a flower pot.

◀ Mike feels that maximizing the flow of light is critical in helping a small home to feel as large as possible. For this reason, he and Elisha chose a glass-panel door rather than a solid one. Small decisions like this can make a big difference.

▲ The open shelving helps keep the space from feeling too boxed-in. Using a shiny material like stainless steel also bounces the light around, which creates a neat effect.

◀ Mike is unusually handy, but he provides a good role model in that he has used this row of base cabinets to demonstrate what is possible with just a couple of hundred dollars in materials. Note the nice alignment of the grain across the bamboo cabinet doors.

▶ Even though this is a fairly modern kitchen, it still feels homey, thanks to small touches, like this set of vintage canisters.

▽ A true modernist, and also a man with a fine appreciation for usable scrap wood, Mike trimmed out the windows with offcuts from the bamboo sheets that he used to build the cabinet doors.

▲ Would you guess that these appliances were purchased used? I wouldn't. Mike and Elisha saved thousands by finding a used appliance dealer who sells newer models — and the warranties are still in effect.

◀ The transition between the concrete countertop and the elevated laminate breakfast bar is highlighted with this monolithic end panel.

◀ Concrete provides the option for a lot of design flexibility — Mike cast these discarded motorcycle brake rotors in place for use as built-in trivets next to the stove.

▼ Mike and Elisha know how to pick their battles: Mike built the base cabinets himself, and then they purchased ready-to-assemble (RTA) wall cabinets from a large retailer at a very reasonable cost.

Top-Notch Organizers at a Reasonable Price

As demand has risen for storage accessories, organization giant, Closetmaid, has decided to expand into the kitchen market, with a positive outcome for homeowners. I was shocked during a recent trip to my local home improvement store when I saw a new line of pullout organizers at really great prices. Named the Procuisine series, it is a big step up from the white-wire line that Closetmaid may be better known for. They feature full-extension sliders, nice-looking chrome plated components, solid wood surfaces, and, in my opinion, the best ratio of value to performance that I've seen. The line includes pull-out trash and recycling containers, roll-out storage trays and drawers in a number of sizes and configurations, and more. A nice thing about these units is that they could be easily incorporated into your kitchen for a low-cost upgrade or they could be the icing on the cake for a full-blown kitchen remodel. Either way, they look to be easy to install in minutes with just a few screws.

While I wouldn't say that the prices are bargain-basement, I would nevertheless like to point out that the retail price you'll pay in your local home store for these items is the same as my wholesale price for comparable items. So, if you are interested in taking the organization up a notch in your new or existing kitchen, you won't find a better value. It is also worth noting that I'm not a Closetmaid spokesman or anything like that — I'm just passing on a good money-saving tip.

Another great source for organizers and supplies (this is especially helpful if you'll be building your own accessories) is Rockler. I recommend taking a look at their pullout and pantry sliders in particular.

Rockler model No. 4WB-1419-52 base-cabinet basket pullout.

Rockler model No. 432-WF-3C wall-cabinet pullout.

Rockler model No. 56907 base-cabinet pullout.

Rockler model No. 5432-05CR base-cabinet pullout.

TILING A BACKSPLASH

Whether you're simply making a few updates to an existing design or starting from scratch with a whole new kitchen, a tile backsplash can be a cost-effective way to add style and value to the finished project. If you're handy, you may consider doing this project yourself to save a few bucks and get the satisfaction of a job well done. As with any type of project, some tile designs are more complex than others, but most do-it-yourselfers should be able to handle a backsplash.

I used glass mosaic tile for the backsplash because it's inexpensive and it doesn't require renting a tile saw, so it streamlines the process even further. While your project will probably vary somewhat from mine, I think the photos illustrate just how simple it can be. The whole project took me about 3 hours, not including a trip to the home center, and it cost around $50 for the whole thing.

Setting Tile

When you're setting the tile, it is not uncommon for some adhesive to squeeze up into the gap between tiles. You'll want to remove this before it sets. I use a putty knife and a wet sponge to make sure all of the joints are clean. The best way to handle this issue is not using too much adhesive in the first place.

Prior to installing the tile, this backsplash area had been painted the same color as the rest of the walls. It wasn't bad, but it didn't add anything to the kitchen design overall, and it was hard to clean. The area above the stove is a potentially messy spot in most kitchens, and an easy-to-clean surface is practically a necessity for this reason.

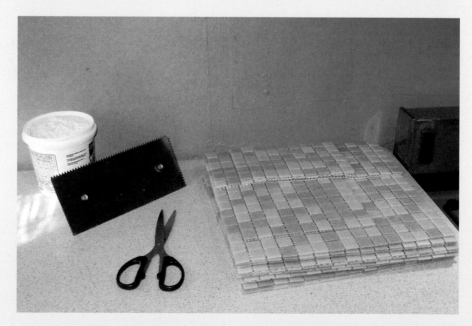

Mosaic tile is available in glass or ceramic, and it comes in sheets that usually measure around 14" x 14" or so. Setting this kind of tile doesn't take much in the way of tools — the sheets can be cut with a pair of scissors — and I try arrange my layouts so I don't have to cut any tiles. You'll want to measure and do a bit of head scratching beforehand so you know how many sheets to buy and how to lay them out.

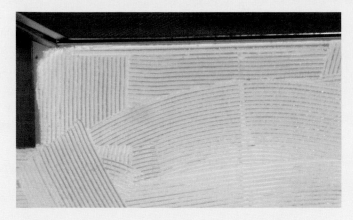

Using the type and size of trowel that is recommended by the manufacturer of the tile and adhesive, I covered the wall with thinset mortar. You have about 20 minutes of open time before the adhesive starts to set up, so you'll need to either work fast or work in smaller sections.

Setting the tile took about an hour. You can see that I left a small gap below the microwave cabinet. This was the result of my decision to start with a full row of tiles below the stove hood, which is a visually prominent spot. This is no problem because I knew I'd be putting some trim along the bottom of the upper cabinets to hide undercabinet lighting, and this would effectively conceal the half-row.

After allowing 24 hours for the tile adhesive to set, I grouted the joints. Grout usually comes in powdered form and can be quickly mixed with water to the consistency of shaving cream. Follow the manufacturer's instructions and you'll do just fine. A rubber float is used to press the grout into the gaps, and a diagonal motion — at an angle to the grout lines — works best.

Once it has been applied, the grout needs to be left to haze over. This will indicate that it is dry enough for you to begin removing the excess grout from the faces of the tiles. If you do this too early, the grout in the joints won't be hard enough and you'll end up pulling it out.

Removing the grout from the tiles is straightforward. A clean, damp sponge does the trick. Depending on the size of the backsplash, this should take between 15 minutes and an hour. You'll need to keep rinsing the sponge so you don't end up just smearing grout all over the place.

After allowing the grout to dry for a day or so, you'll need to protect it with two to three coats of sealer. This takes a few minutes and it will make caring for your new backsplash a snap.

Cabinet Refacing

Let's face it. The idea of building your own kitchen cabinets is beyond most people, but that doesn't mean that everybody but the most hardcore woodworkers fall into the category of helpless. Most people have what it takes to conduct a successful refacing of their existing kitchen cabinets.

Assuming that the layout of the kitchen is okay and that the cabinet boxes are in acceptable condition, refacing is one of the most eco-friendly options available. Less materials are required, next to nothing goes in a landfill, and there are minimal transportation costs to contribute to a large carbon footprint.

The place to begin is, naturally, with the planning. You'll first need to decide what you're able to do. It could be that a simple coat of paint and some new countertops will satisfy you, If so, head to the home center for some paint, call around for countertop estimates, and you'll be ready to go.

Get new doors or re-use old ones? If they're profiled, your best option is to paint them. And new hardware can make a big difference.

If a true refacing is in order, it helps to proceed systematically. I like to begin by removing all the doors and drawers and all the accompanying hardware (i.e., hinges and door pulls). This will give you a good look at the task ahead of you. Most refacing projects require you to cut out strips of veneer and glue them to the exposed areas of the cabinet. This is fairly straightforward. I suggest putting on pieces one at a time, following the existing layout of cabinet parts. That is to say, the ends of the veneer pieces should line up with the joints between the existing parts.

To streamline the process, I start with the horizontal pieces that are "captured" on the ends by vertical pieces. Getting a nice fit on the horizontals will make it easy to align the verticals. It is okay — necessary, even — to cut the veneer pieces a little over wide. The extra material can quickly be trimmed back with a razor blade or veneer trimmer. If the ends aren't flush, you can use a square or a straightedge to guide an exacto knife and cut the veneer in the right place. Once the front faces of the cabinets are done, you can cover up any exposed side panels with either ¼" plywood in the same species that you're using, or sheets of veneer. When the veneer work is complete, it can be stained and varnished as any project would be.

To refurbish the doors, you'll either need to get or make new ones, or if they are flat panel doors, you could veneer the fronts and edges. Local cabinet shops may be able to fabricate new doors for you, or there are a number of other sources that you'll find in the appendix of this book. Just measure the existing doors and you'll have a workable set of measurements for the new doors.

One useful resource for cabinet refacing is Rockler. They offer a custom door and drawer service featuring a number of attractive wood species and styles.

PAINTING EXISTING KITCHEN CABINETS

Make sure that there is no wax, oil, furniture polish, or dirt on the cabinets. In fact, any kind of residue at all can cause problems getting the paint to properly adhere to the cabinets. I recommend scrubbing all the exposed surfaces with Formula 409 (or similar) cleaner and letting everything dry.

You'll also want to remove the doors so you can access all of the areas that will need paint. It's also easier to paint doors when they're sitting on a flat surface than when they're hanging, and it saves you from being crouched down uncomfortably for long periods of time when you paint the base cabinet doors.

The technique you use to apply the paint will depend on the door style and the equipment you have available to you. I have a sprayer and am practiced with its use, so I can spray a set of doors efficiently. If you have one or want to rent one, that's one option. Your other options are a standard bristle brush or a chisel-tip foam brush for flat panel doors. If the doors have any detail at all (raised panels, edge profiles, applied moldings, etc.), your best bet will be to use a bristle brush so you can get into all the nooks and crannies. In any event, I recommend using a semi-gloss paint so everyday spills can be easily wiped off.

Cabinet Construction

Building cabinets using integral toe kicks or separate bases is largely a matter of habit or how your cabinet-making was first learned.

There are advantages to making separate bases.

1. I have made separate bases for years and am used to the process of installing and leveling a series of bases so I can simply set the cabinet boxes on them.

2. Building cabinets with separate bases allows for a slightly more efficient use of material: I can get six cabinet sides out of a sheet of plywood (30" × 24"), whereas I get 4 sides when they're (34½" × 24"). Granted, the offcuts are still usable, but it is nice to be able to crank out a bunch of 30" × 24" pieces.

3. When making the bases, it uses up 4½"-wide scrap.

However, I do find that it is slightly faster to build cabinets with integrated toe kicks but they take me a bit longer to install.

Building Cabinets in Production Runs

When I build a run of cabinets, I determine the required number of parts and make lists of quantities and dimensions. Many of the parts turn out to be identical (i.e., cabinet sides). This helps save time on saw setups.

To illustrate how I plan this out, I'm including my original working notes (see page 82) for a run of 10 base cabinets. I first write out a list of cabinet widths — the heights and depths were all consistent in this case, as they usually are — and I then broke down a list of the size and dimensions of the side and bottom panels.

Assigning a letter to each part, I sketch utilization charts to figure out the quantity of materials I'll need and how many of each size part will fit onto a given sheet of melamine. This makes it easy to start cutting, and it also assures consistency in the size of the parts. I set my fence to 23½" and ripped six sheets to this width. Then, I crosscut the parts to length.

PLANNING RULES OF THUMB:
ESTIMATING MATERIALS QUANTITIES AND
BUDGETING FOR SHEET GOODS
When I'm planning a set of cabinets, I always take the time to do some sketches and list-making to help determine the quantities of materials that I'll need to buy. I like to head into a project confident that I'll

This stack of parts may not look like much now, but it came in the door an hour ago in the form of 4×8 sheets, and soon it will turn into a nice set of base cabinets. You'll notice that I've stacked the side panels in one pile and the cabinet bottoms in another. This makes it easy to grab the sides and drill them with the rows of holes that will be required for holding shelf pegs.

I have a boring machine that drills a row of holes in one motion, and it is invaluable to me since I use it on almost a daily basis. I can bore all of the holes in a pair of cabinet sides in under a minute. But, at $1,000+, it would be hard to justify for most home shops. Another way to drill holes is to make a jig of thin plywood, drill the row of holes in the plywood, then place the jig on the cabinet panel and use the jig to guide your drill.

Base cabinet needed:

sink base	36" w
db	21" w
db	40" w
db	22" w
db	22" w
db	32" w
db	32" w
db	32" w
db	18" w
db	18" w

10 Base cabinets

A- 20 sides $34\frac{1}{2}$" × $23\frac{1}{2}$"

B- 3 botts $30\frac{1}{2}$" × $23\frac{1}{2}$"

C- 2 botts $16\frac{1}{2}$" × $23\frac{1}{2}$"

D- 2 botts $20\frac{1}{2}$" × $23\frac{1}{2}$"

E- 1 bott $38\frac{1}{2}$" × $23\frac{1}{2}$"

F- 1 bott $19\frac{1}{2}$" × $23\frac{1}{2}$"

G- 1 bott $34\frac{1}{2}$" × $23\frac{1}{2}$"

be able to see it through easily rather than be worried about the possibility of running short of materials and having to make additional trips to suppliers, causing me to split the tasks and then unnecessarily repeat some of my setups.

If you're looking for an easy rule of thumb, I've found that I can get 10 base cabinets from 6 sheets of $\frac{3}{4}$" 4×8 melamine-coated particle board, and 3 sheets of melamine-coated MDF. I get decent pricing since I buy in bulk, so for me this works out to about $200 — or $20 per cabinet. Bear in mind that this doesn't include edge-banding, doors, or drawers — we're talking just cabinet boxes. If you're building upper cabinets, you can almost double your yield, so that would be roughly $10 per cabinet. You'll have to spend some money on door and drawer materials, plus the hardware that makes it all work, but I think this gives you a good idea of the kind of savings you'll achieve by building your own cabinets instead of ordering them from a custom cabinet shop.

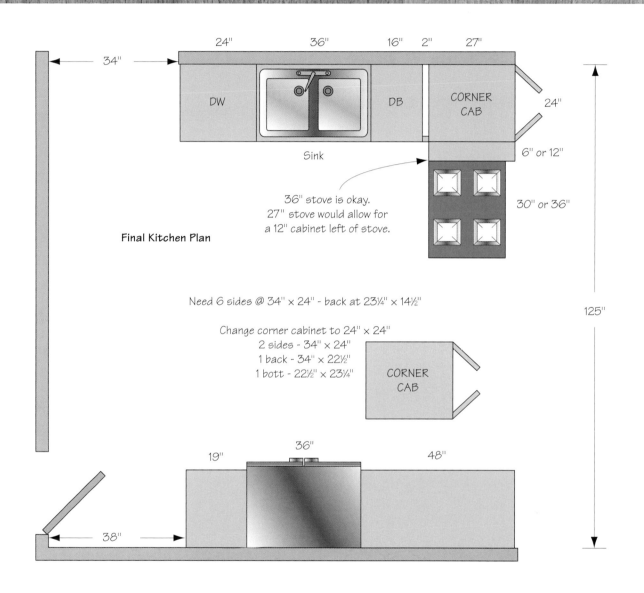

Final Kitchen Plan

34"

24" · 36" · 16" · 2" · 27"

DW

Sink

DB

CORNER CAB

24"

6" or 12"

30" or 36"

125"

36" stove is okay.
27" stove would allow for
a 12" cabinet left of stove.

Need 6 sides @ 34" x 24" - back at 23¼" x 14½"

Change corner cabinet to 24" x 24"
2 sides - 34" x 24"
1 back - 34" x 22½"
1 bott - 22½" x 23¼"

CORNER CAB

19" · 36" · 48"

38"

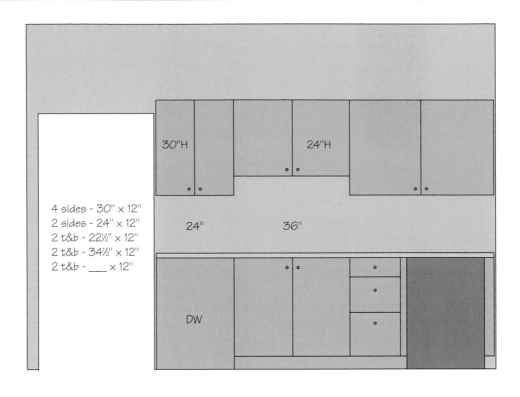

4 sides - 30" × 12"
2 sides - 24" × 12"
2 t&b - 22½" × 12"
2 t&b - 34½" × 12"
2 t&b - ___ × 12"

30"H   24"H

24"   36"

DW

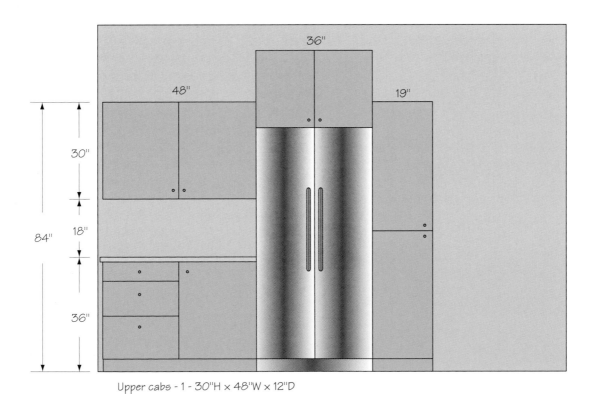

36"

48"   19"

30"

84"   18"

36"

Upper cabs - 1 - 30"H × 48"W × 12"D
2 sides - 30" × 12"
2 t&b - 46½" × 12"

TIMESAVER

When you're building a sink base cabinet, there is generally no need to drill holes to accommodate shelf pegs — the plumbing usually takes up most of the space, so you won't be able to get a shelf in there anyway. That said, there are under-sink organizers that are available. They won't require peg holes either, but at least you'll be able to capitalize on the space rather than just wasting it entirely.

▲ The base cabinets each featured an indented toe-space where their front sides meet the floor. I cut a notch on each cabinet side to create this feature. To speed up the process and to assure consistent results, I trace a 4½" x 3" template in the appropriate spot and make the cutout using a jigsaw.

▲ It is important to think in pairs because you'll need a right and a left side for each cabinet!

▲ The ¼" thick cabinet back can then be secured with glue and nails or screws. If you're using melamine, you'll want to use a melamine-specific adhesive made by Titebond or RooGlue.

A note on squaring cabinets: The old standby of measuring diagonals never goes out of style, but I've also found another method that seems to work well for cabinet assembly, and that is to simply start with a square cabinet back and, as you're securing it to the cabinet, make sure the sides and bottom of the cabinet are flush with the edges of the back. You are basically using the cabinet back as a layout tool, and a carefully assembled cabinet will square itself. The trick is making sure that the backs are square, which hasn't been a problem for me since I cut out the panels using a table saw sled that cuts perpendicular to the blade.

◄ Now that the sides are finished, assembly can proceed. Working on a bench top or some sawhorses, I use a quick-clamp to hold a bottom panel in alignment with one of the cabinet sides. The 4½" x 3" template can also be used as a spacer to help indicate where to place screws on the outside of the cabinet sides. This is a lot quicker than measuring each time. I also use it on the inside of the side as a way of showing me where to position the bottom panel. The process is repeated on the other side of the cabinet to create a U-shaped assembly.

This run of base cabinets — which still need edge-banding on the faces of the sides and bottom and some reinforcing strips along its top — is mostly completed. It only took a few hours.

I use the 4½" x 3" cutout spacer to indicate where to position the fasteners that go through the back and into the back edge of the bottom panel. Make sure to position the fasteners at least a couple of inches in from the edges of the panel to prevent blow-outs in the side and bottom panels.

Designing and Building Drawers

Building drawers can get a little tricky because it requires you to think in multiple units rather than just building things one at a time. Fortunately, taking the time to do your homework early on will pay big dividends later. The process will go quickly and smoothly and you'll be able to relax because you'll know that your dimensions all check out and that you have enough material on hand.

You can build drawers out of solid wood or plywood, depending on your preference and your budget. Joinery is of course another option: Dovetails remain the gold standard, but there are a number of other acceptable joinery options that I'll cover, too.

Before you go any further in your planning, you'll need to make a few decisions. You'll need to know what type of material you'll be using (mostly because you'll need to know its thickness), and what type of drawer slide you'll be using, because different styles and models require different clearances between the drawer and the cabinet sides. That information should be supplied when you purchase the drawer slides — any catalog or website should list this for you, and if you don't see it, ask.

Once you've decided these things, and once you have the cabinet dimensions (the interior dimensions are the ones that matter) you can go ahead and plan your drawers. There are a couple of goals here: One is to generate a cut list, and the other is to get a clear idea on how much material you should purchase ahead of time so that you can build all your drawers at once. If you're not comfortable doing large "production style" runs, you could always build your drawers one at a time, but this will naturally slow down the process. And, you'll still need to jump through the same planning hoops, so there's really no savings.

This example will utilize ½"- thick birch plywood (I'll edge-band the top edge, for a more finished look), K&V drawer slides — which are side-mount slides that feature a self-closing mechanism. They require ½" of clearance on each side of the drawer. Elsewhere in this book, I'll use some Accuride under-mount self-closing slides, so you'll see that detailed there.

Each drawer has three dimensions: Depth, width and height. When I say "depth", I am referring to the front-to-back measurement of the drawer and not the vertical measurement (which is referred to as height). I could use the word length instead of depth, but "length" doesn't make as much sense to me intuitively as "depth". In your own projects, just stick with whatever terms work for you. Calculating depth is easy — I usually make the drawers ½" less than the

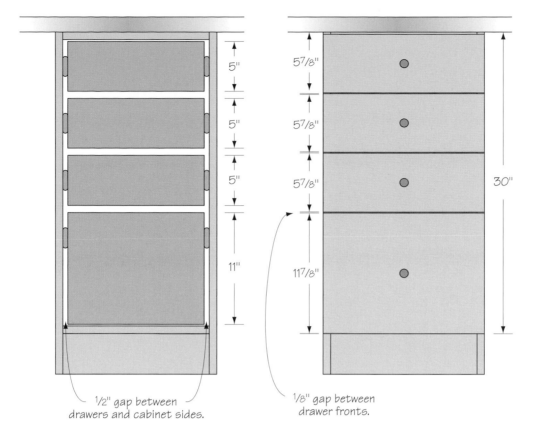

5"

5"

5"

11"

1/2" gap between
drawers and cabinet sides.

5⁷⁄₈"

5⁷⁄₈"

5⁷⁄₈"

11⁷⁄₈"

30"

1/8" gap between
drawer fronts.

depth of the cabinet interior. The width when using these slides is determined by subtracting 1" from the interior measurement of the cabinet. The height is a bit trickier — you need to know how big the drawer fronts will be, and then count back from there. To help me figure this out, I usually do a sketch of the cabinet, as viewed from the front. In this case, I have a 30" cabinet, which I've divided into three equally sized drawers above one large one. This yields 6", 6", 6" and 12" drawer fronts, but these measurements must be shrunk a bit to accommodate the need for a small gap between each drawer front. Plan on ⅛" for this. This gives me drawer fronts of 5⁷⁄₈", 5⁷⁄₈", 5⁷⁄₈" and 11⁷⁄₈". When it comes to sizing the drawers, I always make them smaller than the drawer fronts — the exact size isn't too critical. In this case, 5", 5", 5" and 10½" works out fine.

My cabinet interior measured 14½"-wide by 23¼"-deep by 28½"-high, so I needed to build drawers with the following dimensions:

3 @ 22¾" deep × 13½"-wide × 5"-high
1 @ 22¾"-deep × 13½"-wide × 10¹⁄₂"-high

This list allowed me to make a cutting list that indicates the sizes and quantities of the parts that will make up each drawer. In this example, I've used ½" stock that will be joined with pocket-screw joinery (butt joints and Kreg screws). The Kreg screws will be hidden on the back side of the drawer and by the drawer front. (See Pocket-Screw Joinery illustration on page 88.) Having decided on the joinery method beforehand is critical because dovetail or miter joints, for example, would require cutting parts of different sizes. Because I am using ½" stock and butt joints, I simply subtract 1" (2 × ½", the thickness of the drawer sides) from the overall width of the drawer.

Here's the cut list:

6 drawer sides:	22¾" × 5"
6 drawer front/backs:	12½" × 5"
2 drawer sides:	22¾" × 10½"
2 drawer front/backs:	12½" × 10½"
4 drawer bottoms:	13" × 23"
	(cut from ¼" stock)

The last thing to do is figure out how much material I'll need for all these parts. To do this, I make a quick sketch that helps me to visualize exactly how I'll cut each part from my supply of stock. Here I used 4×8 sheets of plywood, but the method is the same with solid-wood planks. When cutting out drawer parts, I always run the grain horizontally. Also, I often have scraps that I can use up for some of the drawer parts, so I take those into consideration and subtract their future yield from the total number of parts that I'll need to cut from fresh material.

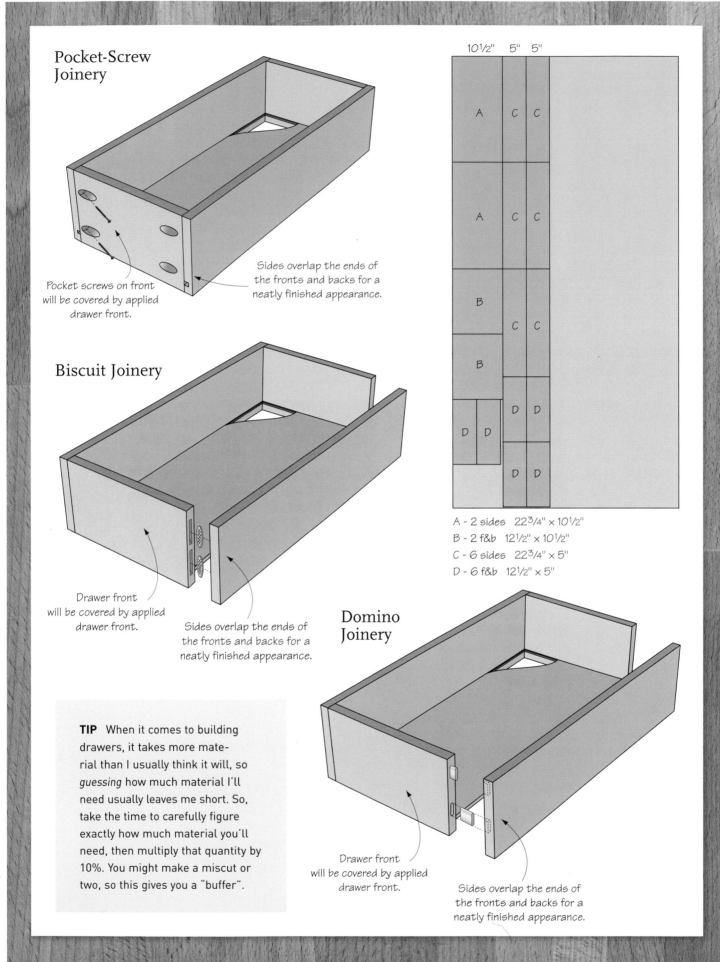

Pocket-Screw Joinery

Pocket screws on front will be covered by applied drawer front.

Sides overlap the ends of the fronts and backs for a neatly finished appearance.

Biscuit Joinery

Drawer front will be covered by applied drawer front.

Sides overlap the ends of the fronts and backs for a neatly finished appearance.

Domino Joinery

Drawer front will be covered by applied drawer front.

Sides overlap the ends of the fronts and backs for a neatly finished appearance.

10½" 5" 5"

A
C C

A
C C

B
C C

B

D D
D D

D D

A - 2 sides   22¾" × 10½"
B - 2 f&b   12½" × 10½"
C - 6 sides   22¾" × 5"
D - 6 f&b   12½" × 5"

TIP When it comes to building drawers, it takes more material than I usually think it will, so *guessing* how much material I'll need usually leaves me short. So, take the time to carefully figure exactly how much material you'll need, then multiply that quantity by 10%. You might make a miscut or two, so this gives you a "buffer".

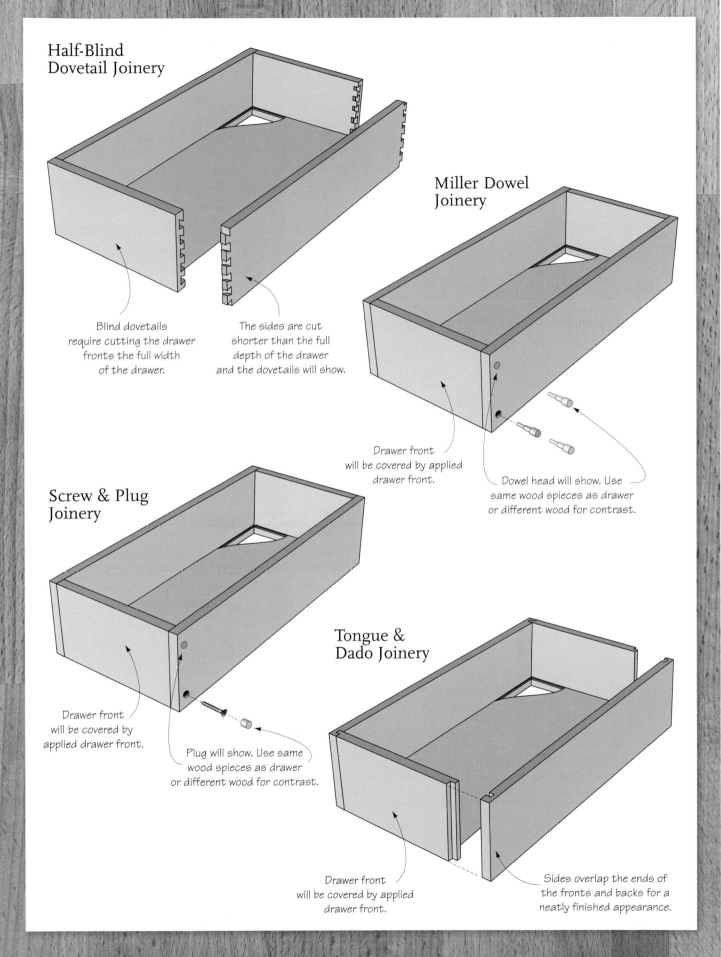

Half-Blind Dovetail Joinery

Blind dovetails require cutting the drawer fronts the full width of the drawer.

The sides are cut shorter than the full depth of the drawer and the dovetails will show.

Miller Dowel Joinery

Drawer front will be covered by applied drawer front.

Dowel head will show. Use same wood spieces as drawer or different wood for contrast.

Screw & Plug Joinery

Drawer front will be covered by applied drawer front.

Plug will show. Use same wood spieces as drawer or different wood for contrast.

Tongue & Dado Joinery

Drawer front will be covered by applied drawer front.

Sides overlap the ends of the fronts and backs for a neatly finished appearance.

Finishing Cabinet Doors

Even if you're experienced and confident with finishing, handling a whole set of cabinet doors poses some unique challenges. In my experience, it is beneficial to apply the finishes — particularly stains — to all of the components at once in order to achieve consistent results. Even a small difference in application (i.e., how long a stain is allowed to penetrate before it is wiped off), can produce a noticeable difference in the finish, and weather differences can easily affect how quickly a stain soaks in, so even if you wait the same amount of time prior to wiping away the excess, the stain may not be absorbed in the same way from one day to the next. This probably won't be an issue if you're simply clear-coating your components.

Sometimes I work with a complex finish that requires three or more coats of stain, and each coat provides, frankly, a new opportunity to screw things up. So I try as hard as possible to work consistently at every stage.

The other challenge posed by a large run of cabinet doors is figuring out how to store them. Few of us have the space to lay out thirty or more cabinet doors, and even if we did, every horizontal surface would be occupied and the shop would be effectively out of commission while finishes dry. Here are a few strategies to consider to help you manage this task most efficiently:

1. A tiered baker's rack. I bought a used one for $20. You could probably build something similar with 2×2s and scrap wood for little cost.

2. Rockler has introduced a product which consists of hooks that lock into the 35mm hinge holes so the doors can be hung "clothesline" style on a cable.

3. I once saw a photo of a great-looking fold-out drying rack that mounts to the wall. You could make this in under and hour and it just might be what you need.

I have a drying rack with one additional advantage that is worth mentioning: Once it's loaded up, you can wheel it into another room (a closet would even provide enough space) and continue to work without worrying about sawdust getting on the doors and into the finish. This is handy since most folks (myself included) don't have a dedicated finishing room. It is disruptive to have the whole shop down for the count while you're waiting for a finish to dry.

A baker's rake is perfect for storing doors, drawer fronts and loose cabinet sides while the finish dries.

HE AIN'T HEAVY, HE'S MY CABINET

A base cabinet with a full set of drawers can be heavy, especially when you're using ¾"- thick material for the cabinet sides and back. I work alone in my shop, so having a couple of carts on hand is essential for moving cabinets around during the assembly process.

For certain tasks, drawer installation, for example, you may want to consider placing cabinets directly on the floor instead of on a bench top because you won't have to worry about safely moving a big, heavy cabinet onto the floor when you're done.

And when you're ready for moving day, I can't say enough about the merits of getting a helper. I used to tough it out and do all of the loading and unloading myself, but needless to say, I learned the hard way that it just isn't worth the hassle. Two people can easily move a whole kitchen's worth of cabinets in just a few hours, so I'm happy to pay somebody to help out.

Still not convinced? Here's a couple of good reasons to get help with the heavy stuff:

- Reduce the risk of personal injury
- Reduce the risk of damage to the cabinets
- Reduce the risk of damaging the job site, i.e., dings on door casings, floors, etc.
- Allows you to work more productively and for longer stretches of time
- You won't wake up as sore the next day and you can actually enjoy the process

Pull-Out Pantry Design & Construction

A pull-out pantry was to be located next to the refrigerator and it was going to be accessed from only one side. This is because the cabinet is noticeably shallower than the refrigerator and the white oak panel, so the pull-out couldn't be accessed easily from the refrigerator-side of the unit. For this reason, I built a pull-out with a back on the same side as the refrigerator.

I used ½" plywood for most of the unit and attached a ¼" back. (These material choices helped keep the weight down.) To stiffen the shelves, and to keep items from falling off them, I added a ½"- thick lip along the front edge of each shelf. This ensured that they wouldn't sag over time. In terms of construction, the unit was essentially a large box with a back screwed on. To make the finishing process easier, I didn't fully assemble the unit until it had been lacquered. Once the finish was dry, I assembled the unit. This saved me a lot of time. If I had installed the shelves prior to finishing, that would have created a number of small, hard-to-reach areas that would have taken a lot more time and effort to finish.

Installing the slides into the cabinet was easy (although I did need to get some help moving this unusually tall and heavy cabinet). The key to installing the slides is to place the cabinet on saw horses so that I could access the bottom of the pull-out. (Before I attached the slides, I had been wondering how I'd accomplish this. I looked around my shop and saw a pair of sawhorses against the wall — the solution was obvious.)

I used Accuride 301 series slides, which I highly recommend for this purpose. They are very forgiving, in that they didn't require much in the way of precise alignments. The critical factor was that they needed to be set flush to the front of the cabinet so that the front of the pullout would be flush with the front of the cabinet. They also needed to be parallel to the cabinet sides but there was no particular spacing required in terms of their side-to-side positioning. Once the slides were screwed to the cabinet bottom, I lifted the pull-out into place and centered it side-to-side within the cabinet. (This pullout was 15¼" wide, and the opening was 16½" wide, so I had a gap of ⅝" on each side.)

I extended the slides a couple of inches and aligned the front of the pull-out with the front edge of the slides, then I secured the slides to the bottom of the pull-out from below. This is where the sawhorses were essential. I extended the pull-out completely and made sure the gap on the sides was still ⅝" — this let me know that the pull-out was parallel to the cabinet sides and would slide easily. I then screwed the

slides to the bottom of the pull-out along the back edge and tested the movement. I installed a standard side-mount slide on the top of the pull-out to keep it stable once it was loaded up. I mounted the slide to the cabinet panel prior to putting the panel in place. The slide required ½" of clearance above the pullout, so I made sure to allow for that when I positioned the panel above the pullout. Once the panel was screwed in place, I extended the pullout and screwed the slide to the top it.

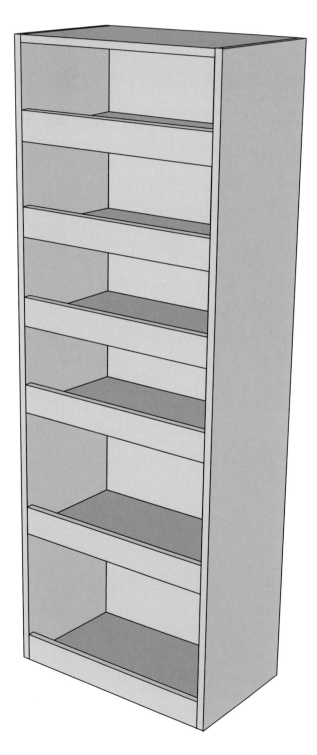

STEP ONE First, I installed the lower guides in the bottom of the cabinet.

STEP TWO I set the pullout inside the cabinet on the lower pullout hardware and centered the pullout in the cabinet. The weight of the cabinet allowed me to pull the shelf unit forward without it sliding out of place on the hardware. I pulled the unit out about 5". To attach the pullout to the bottom slides, I installed the front screws first, then pulled the unit out to install the back screws.

STEP THREE By first installing the upper drawer slide on the bottom of the top shelf, I was able to locate the shelf at exactly the correct height in the cabinet.

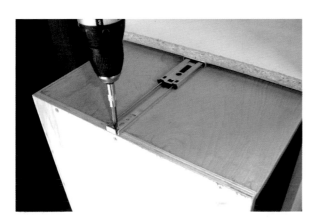

STEP FOUR I extended the drawer slide until it reached the front of the pullout, made sure the top of the shelf unit was centered in the cabinet and installed the front screw. After testing the operation of the pullout, I fully extended it and installed the back screws in the drawer slide.

STEP FIVE There is plenty of storage space above the pullout for the lesser-used items in your kitchen.

PULL-OUT PANTRY VERSION 2

Here's an alternative pull-out pantry design that varies somewhat from the first one I presented. This design allows access from either side. Basically, this pullout consists of a series of "drawers" that are spaced at convenient heights and secured to a matching set of vertical end panels. Once assembled, the unit is both light-weight and sturdy. In this case, I used Accuride 9301 slides with a bottom-mount option.

▲ When assembling units that are large, I use what I can to make a bench (note my table saw serving as a "bench").

◀ The shelves are attached to the sides of the pullout using screws. This is an effective and quick way to assemble this pullout.

WORKING IN PRODUCTION RUNS

More than most other projects, kitchens will offer you the double-sided opportunity-and-challenge of building identical items. Such work sequences are generally called "production runs". If you haven't done much of this before, it may not hurt to build one item of a series beforehand just to reassure yourself that it'll work and to double-check your planning and techniques. For example, if you have to build a set of ten drawers, you may find that it helps your confidence to simply build one first and make sure that it works out as planned. This also allows you to catch any mistakes or discrepancies early and avoid having an entire set of ten that didn't turn out at planned. You can then go ahead and build the other nine as a production run.

Once you're ready to do an entire run, planning is critical, and good planning means knowing what materials you'll need and how much of them. Nothing spoils productivity like having to leave the shop and head back to the store. And be forewarned: If you're just guesstimating, drawers in particular always seem to require more material than you would think.

A helpful mental approach is to think in terms of components rather than finished items. You can focus more on "how many sides/fronts/backs/bottoms" do I need. You'll find yourself multiplying by two quite often, because each drawer has two sides, and the front and back are often identical in size.

Because working in production runs can be confusing initially, the most helpful tip that I can offer is to break down the process into individual steps. For example:

1. Rip drawer stock into 6" widths from 4×8 × ½" plywood
2. Using a dado blade, cut a groove for the drawer bottoms
3. Crosscut the stock to finished lengths on the miter saw
4. Edge-band the top edges of the parts
5. Assemble the front and two sides into a U-shape
6. Measure for drawer bottoms and cut them out
7. Insert the drawer bottoms and fasten the final drawer back in place

This may seem unnecessary, but I find that breaking down the process keeps me moving swiftly and not being so overwhelmed with the number of parts and assemblies. With practice it gets a lot easier. The stack of drawers that you see here took me under an hour from start to finish (not including the clear-coating). Granted, the joinery was quick, just glue and nails, but you can see that the method pays off. And the more finished units you're trying to end up with, the more beneficial the time savings becomes.

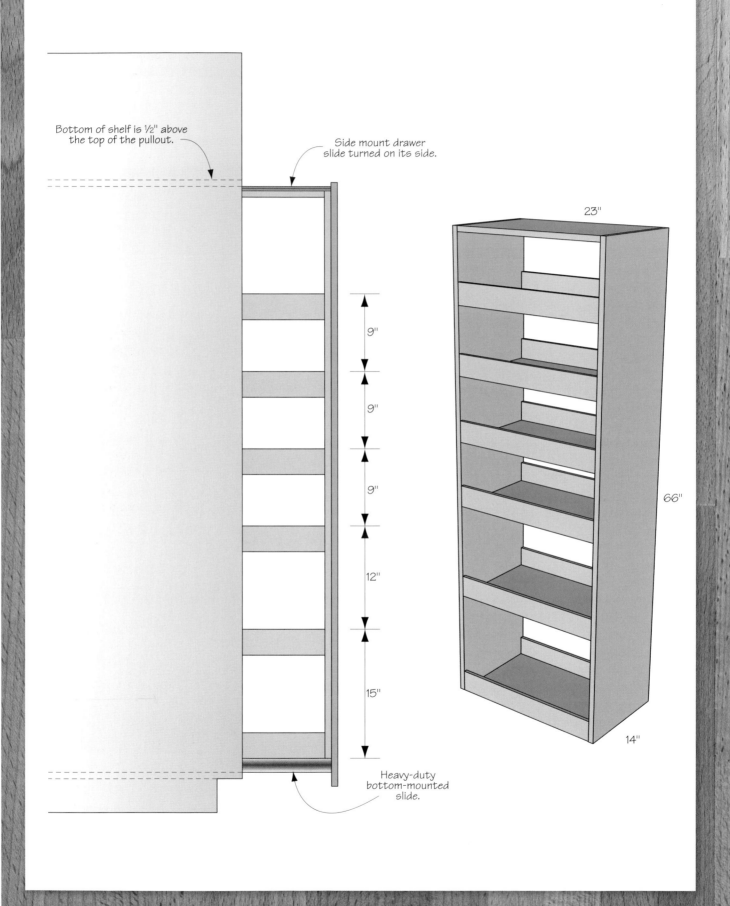

Bottom of shelf is ½" above
the top of the pullout.

Side mount drawer
slide turned on its side.

9"

9"

9"

12"

15"

Heavy-duty
bottom-mounted
slide.

23"

66"

14"

Cabinet Doors and Drawer Fronts with Continuous Horizontal Grain

I've built a lot of kitchen cabinets in the past few years which feature flat panel doors, and it has become trendy to run the grain horizontally. To do this well, you'll need to do a bit of planning so the grain runs continuously from one cabinet door to the next. Not taking the time to do this defeats the purpose: Instead of getting a sleek and flowing effect, you'll have a mish-mash of grain patterns that is pretty unattractive.

There are a couple of tricks to streamlining this process, and a couple of caveats, as well. For one thing, you'll be limited to runs of 96" (the length of a sheet of plywood). This probably won't cause you to alter your dimensions, but it is something to be aware of from the outset. If you'll need to accommodate a longer run, then keep reading: I have a strategy that will help.

Make a sketch of the whole kitchen and assign a letter to each door. You'll need to account for things like cabinet end panels and filler strips so that the grain flows across them too. This will make it easy to compose a list of all of the various parts you'll need. The sketch helps me to think more clearly because I'm used to cutting out doors where the grain runs vertically — orienting the grain horizontally changes everything. This process can be confusing when you're in the heat of the moment, so planning ahead will help to simplify things. Once you have a list, you can look it over and identify the common dimensions — in this case, I had a lot of 30"- wide panels, a couple of 34"- wide ones, and some that measured 24". Getting

a sense for how many pieces you have of a particular size is handy because you'll need to rip plywood sheets to these widths, and you'll need to know how many strips to rip and to which dimensions (these strips are then crosscut on a table saw sled to their finished lengths). To make this clear, I then create a second set of sketches to show me how best to utilize my materials. This will also clarify how much material you'll need, which may have been a bit mysterious up until this point.

Running the grain horizontally tends to produce a bit more scrap material, unless you can plan carefully and alter your dimensions to use up the offcuts. You may also just get lucky. Either way, this can help you to make sure you're budgeting enough material (and consequently, money). If you find yourself with some extra material, well, you've got the makings of another great project.

It is worth pointing out that this kitchen had a cabinet run which was too long to fit on one panel, and the grain would thus be disrupted. I addressed this by choosing a natural breaking point to introduce a different sheet of plywood and by choosing a sheet of plywood that matched as closely as possible. I made sure to purchase my plywood from the same unit with this in mind. In this case, a natural breaking point came between the doors labeled P and Q, or R and S — the shift in the cabinet heights meant that the eye was already likely to be jogging around a bit right there, so a change in the grain pattern would be likely to go unnoticed. However, choosing a second sheet of plywood that mirrors the first is still the best solution.

When a cabinet requires drawer fronts instead of a door, I cut out a panel as if I were making a door. This ensures that it has the same continuous grain characteristics as the adjacent panels (i.e., doors, end panels, filler strips, etc.). Then I crosscut that panel into drawer fronts of the required widths. I make sure to label them from top to bottom and I store them in the same order to ensure that they don't get mixed up. However, if they get mixed up, use your marks to sort them out.

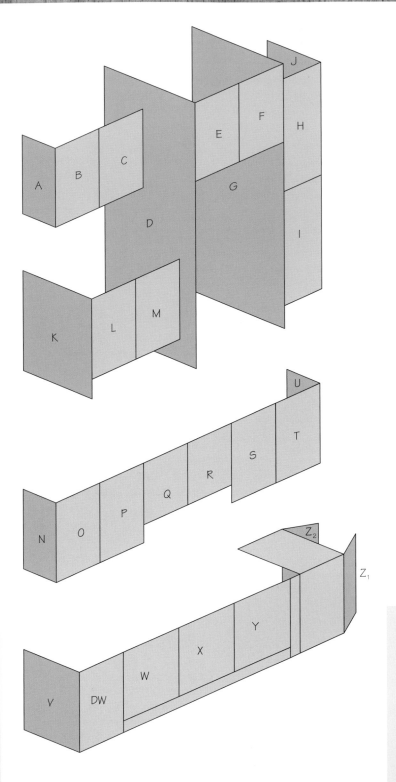

A - 12¼" × 30" end panel

B - 24" × 30" door

C - 24" × 30" door

D - 28" × 96" fridge panel

E - 18" × 24" door

F - 18" × 24" door

G - 28" × 96" fridge panel

H - 18" × 40" door

I - 18" × 40" door

J - 23¼" × 84" side panel

K - 24" × 34" end panel

L - 24" × 30" door

M - 24" × 30" door

N - 12¼" × 30" end panel

O - 12¼" × 30" door

P - 12" × 30" door

Q - 18" × 24" door

R - 18" × 24" door

S - 21" × 30" door

T - 21" × 30" door

U - 12¼" × 30" door

V - 24" × 34" end panel

W - 18" × 30" door

X - 18" × 30" door

Y - 16" × 30" drawer fronts*

Z_1 - 12" × 30" door

Z_2 - 12" × 30" door

TIP If you can find them, using sheet goods that are 97" x 49" instead of exactly 4x8 makes a difference because all of those saw kerfs can add up. A 97" sheets lets me get four 24"- wide panels, whereas a 96"- long sheet would only allow for 3, with a scrap that is about 23½"- long. That is still big enough to be useful, but if you were planning on getting four panels, you'll be making a trip back for a fourth sheet. Either way, good planning before you cut will help you to know that you have enough material on hand.

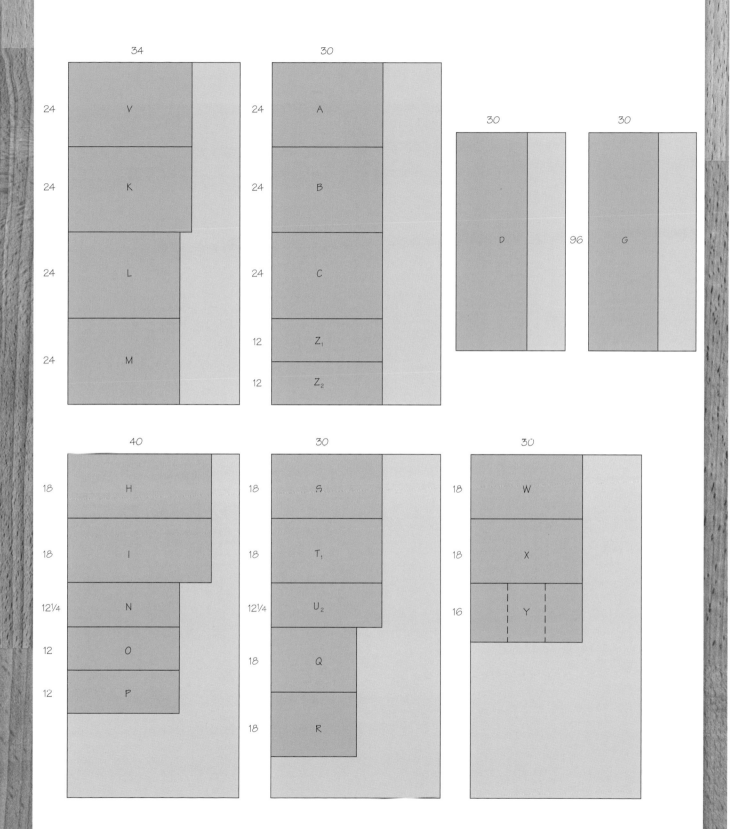

Note: There will be lots of scrap, so plan for this in the budget.

A QUICK AND EASY WAY TO DRILL 35MM HOLES

Most cabinet doors are attached with European-style (35mm cup) hinges. This means you'll need to drill a couple of holes in each door. Some people use a drill press for this, which works great if you have a fence and maybe even a couple of stops, but when the belt broke on my drill press and I couldn't find a replacement that would get me back in business that same day, I came up with another method.

This simple fixture provides a way of drilling a hole a uniform distance from the side and top and bottom edges of the door. It is useful because, in my experience, the time-consuming part of this process is laying out the exact location for each hole and this fixture eliminates that task. Drilling the hole is quick and easy, whether you're using a drill press or a hand-drill and the fixture. (Using the hand drill, it's not difficult to bore the hole perpendicular to the door panel.)

There's no need to clamp the fixture in place — that would waste time. I set the fixture in place and press the drill bit into the hole in the fixture to mark the location on the door. When the fixture has been removed you can drill the hole in a matter of seconds.

The placement of the hole will vary depending on the hinges that you're using. I usually place the center of the hole 7⁄8" from the edge and about 4" from the top and 4" from the bottom. The location of the holes is up to you, but 3"- 4" will work 95% of the time.

Note: A 1⅜" Forstner bit works fine, and it may be less expensive than a 35mm, so shop around a little.

Hanging Wall Cabinets

Although I've hung a lot of wall cabinet alone, I have to admit that having an assistant is the best way to do this — it speeds things up and you can relax in the knowledge that your very safety isn't in jeopardy. I also recommend using a set of cabinet jacks, or failing that, a milk crate and a pile of shim stock. Assuming that you have these bases covered, choosing the right fastener is the next step in the process. Your choice of fastener will be largely determined by the composition of the wall.

- Standard wood-framed walls with drywall or lath-and-plaster

I use 3" washer-head screws because they won't pull through the back of a cabinet. Drywall screws are generally disdained by the pros because they may not be able to provide the shear-strength that this application requires.

- Steel studs

I recommend No. 10 self-tapping sheet metal screws. They are really beefy and should handle the job just fine. I've heard of installers who double them up at the tops of the cabinets to reinforce the connection. Nothing wrong with that.

- Concrete block and brick

I use hammer-set fasteners because they are quick, strong and simple. They require a hole to be drilled with a masonry bit, so you'll need to make sure you're equipped with the right sized bit before you get started. Tapcon screws are another choice. The screws come with the correct size masonry drill bit. You simply drill a hole in the brick or concrete block wall and install the screw in that hole.

In terms of the number of fasteners that you'll use for each cabinet, this is largely a judgment call. The cabinets may be heavy to begin with, and they may be called upon to hold a couple of hundred pounds more once they've been loaded up, so erring on the side of caution and overdoing it is perfectly reasonable here. I use at least 6 fasteners, and often as many as 12 for a larger cabinet. As a rule of thumb, I put at least three fasteners into each stud.

When you're using screws, I recommend square drive heads — they are much easier to drive than Phillips-head screws and you won't have to worry about stripping out the screw head.

For a completely finished look, screw heads can be countersunk and hidden with self-adhesive covers. These are available in white melamine and also a variety of real-wood veneers from Fastcap.

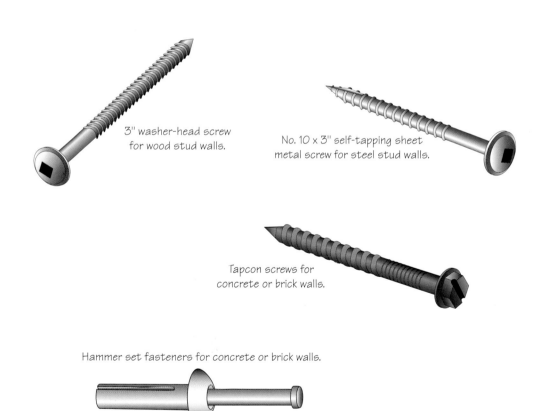

3" washer-head screw for wood stud walls.

No. 10 x 3" self-tapping sheet metal screw for steel stud walls.

Tapcon screws for concrete or brick walls.

Hammer set fasteners for concrete or brick walls.

04

CASE STUDIES

Szykula Kitchen

This is an example of a kitchen in a brand-new home. The home is quite large, over 8,000 sq. ft., so space was not at a premium. The area reserved for the kitchen opened into a great room and an adjoining dining area, making it feel even larger. It was nicely anchored by a standard L-shaped layout against the back walls, but we did need to do a couple of things to help define the kitchen area. One easy strategy was to confine the travertine flooring to the kitchen only. The rest of the house featured hardwood flooring, so this created a clear visual contrast that makes for an unambiguous use of space.

To delineate the spaces further, we positioned a bar area at the edge of the kitchen. This created a transition between the areas reserved for food preparation and for hanging out. We reinforced this distinction by raising the bar area's countertop up 6". Structurally, the bar was created by placing a row of cabinets against a pony wall built by the general contractor. It was pre-wired for outlets on both the front and back sides. It provided a stable place to anchor cabinets.

It is worth mentioning that the end panel on the west side of the bar area needed to be designed differently because it had to trim out the edge of the pony wall. The back side of the bar was covered by a panel which I built as a single unit. It could have been constructed on-site out of pre-finished parts. This reflects my own preference for working in the shop where I

have a full suite of tools at my disposal, rather than on a job site, which can be a hectic environment that is not quite as conducive to efficient work. The radiused countertop had an overhang of 10" at its deepest point. This was supported by a pair of brackets as per the instructions of the countertop fabricators.

The rest of the kitchen layout was not designed around any of the standard rules of thumb (the work triangle or task zones, for example) but simply sought to provide a great deal of workspace with generous amounts of storage and all the major appliances and water within a convenient distance to each other. To this end, the sink, microwave, cooktop and dishwasher are located nearly adjacent to one another, with the refrigerator located along the east wall so that it would be equally convenient to someone simply popping into the kitchen to grab a cold drink or the like. The sink was centered below a window, which is a classic element in most kitchen layout strategies.

Aesthetically, the kitchen is basic: Alder cabinets with a dark stain and an attractive but fairly neutral granite countertop are the main visual elements. This was done to set a strong tone for the space without being overly bold and stealing attention away from one of the most attractive features of the home (a stunning view of the valley below this hilltop home). The kitchen needed to look appropriately grand for its setting but not steal the show.

As a cabinetmaker, I've been called in many times to retrofit cabinets for people who wanted or needed to install a new fridge and had problems fitting it in. In this case, we planned for a 2½"- high trim strip below the fridge cabinet. This was done so it could be removed if extra height was needed in the future.

Another unique feature in this kitchen was the way we handled the cabinetry below the cooktop. Many kitchen designs call for a couple of large drawers below a cooktop, and this can indeed be a handy place to store pots and pans. In this case, that wasn't going to work. The homeowner didn't want the visual clutter of a hood, so the contractor needed to install a downdraft fan below the cooktop. This bulky item didn't leave any room for drawers, so a pair of cabinet doors with a false front above it were the best way to get some use of the remaining space.

And while we're on the topic of cooktops, it pays to plan ahead and chose your cooktop before the cabinets are built. In this case, the homeowner hadn't chosen his cooktop by the time we needed to get started building the cabinets, so I designed the cabinet so it could accommodate whatever cooktop he eventually chose. Some cooktops hang past the edge of the countertop and feature a control panel that comes down as much as 4" or 5" on the cabinet, while others are inset completely into the countertop. In this case, I built a cabinet with a 7"- high panel across its top that provided a couple of options. If the owner chose a drop-down cooktop, we could cut the panel as per the manufacturer's instructions, and if he didn't, the area could be dressed up with a non-operational drawer

front that would line up with the adjacent drawer fronts with the doors below. Either way, the finished look would be fine.

This project also illustrates a useful tip related to designing center islands. The island was constructed using a number of modular cabinets that were fastened to each other. I find this approach makes for a unit that is much easier to work with — instead of having to worry about getting 6 people together on moving day and fretting about having adequate doorway clearances and the like. It's easy to carry in a half dozen smaller cabinets and screw them together to create a strong and attractive assembly. I used a row of three cabinets side-by-side and another row behind them which faced the opposite direction. I covered the ends with panels that I attached from inside the cabinet with screws. To ensure that the parts would go together smoothly on site, I took the time to pre-fit them in the shop. It's nice to walk onto a job-site with confidence rather than trepidation. Eliminating any unforeseen snags goes a long way to easing the workload on installation day. To anchor the whole thing to the floor, I usually fasten a couple of 2×4s to the subfloor and screw the island to them, but in this case, I secured a large angle bracket to the floor in each corner of the island and screwed the brackets to the cabinets. The result was an island that looked great and wouldn't budge.

My first visit to the job site was early on — it wasn't even closed in yet — as evidenced by the puddle on the floor. It was neat to see the project take shape before our eyes, and being there helped me envision the best layout for the space

I use a multiple-spindle boring machine to drill the peg holes in the cabinet sides.

The sides of the base cabinets had to be notched at the bottom to form the toe kicks. I used a 4½" x 3" block as a template.

The sides must be fabricated with right and left sides.

I used a right-angle clamp to keep the parts aligned while I fastening them together. I also use the 4½" template as a guide block so I know where to place the nails and screws that hold the cabinets together.

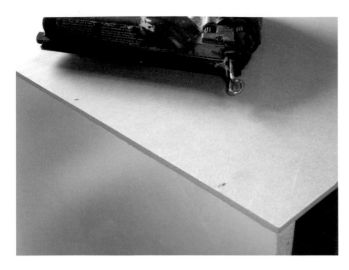

The backs are glued and nailed in place. I use a melamine-specific adhesive to ensure a strong bond.

Here are the base cabinets, lined up like a row of soldiers going into battle.

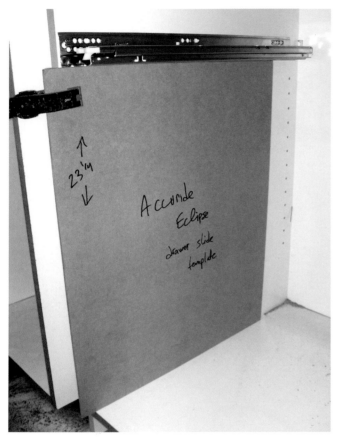

To position the drawer slides, I clamp a template into place. This is faster than measuring, and it doesn't require me to lay the cabinet on its side.

I like to mock-up each kitchen in my shop so I can foresee any problems that might arise during the installation.

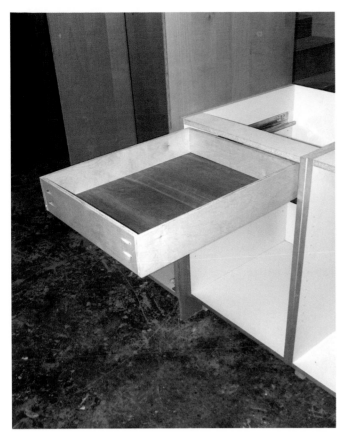

▲ Delivery day! We had to cope with some snow, but the driveway served as a reasonable staging area nonetheless.

◀ The full-extension soft-close slides are a must for a high-end kitchen like this.

▲ I had two assistants for this installations (we also had four bathrooms and a laundry room on this project), and many hands did indeed make for light work.

◀ The early part of the installation moved quickly. The cabinets are set into their approximate positions. The consequent fine-tuning can take a while.

The walls and floor were right-on in terms of being level — this is not always the case! It helped the installation to go very smoothly.

The tile-setters didn't need to run the tiles all the way to the back wall because cabinets were going to be placed there. This saved them a bit of time and effort.

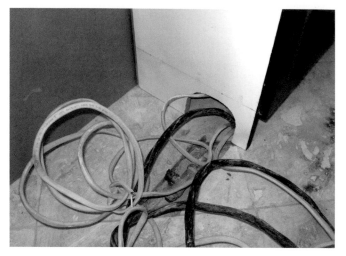

This cabinet base had to be notched to allow a cluster of cables to be run. You can see the gas valve, to which we'll need to provide access by cutting a hole in a cabinet bottom.

The upper cabinets went in quickly thanks to a pair of adjustable cabinet jacks.

The bar area was created by setting a row of base cabinets against a pony wall provided by the contractor. The wall was wired for electrical outlets on the front and back.

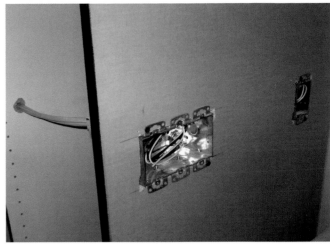

▲ Outlets and switches can be located in the sides of cabinets. However, our building code doesn't allow us to leave exposed cables loose inside a cabinet, so we needed to box in this small portion of the cabinet interior.

◀ Inside corners are areas where two runs of cabinetry intersect at a right angle. They need to be planned to make sure that doors and drawers have room to operate properly. In this case, a pair of filler strips were used to create the necessary clearance.

▲ Getting the appliances installed goes a long way towards helping the kitchen to feel finished.

◀ Two steps forward, one step back. The cabinets were in, but the rest of the house was still messy and this spilled over into the kitchen. Progress doesn't always look like progress.

To anchor the center island to the floor, I secured a large angle bracket in each corner. This required drilling a hole in the cabinet bottom, but this was easy to cover up later.

Drilling the hole provided a way to access the hammer-set masonry anchor and establish a rock-solid connection.

Getting the microwave and the oven installed was a rather time-consuming but straightforward job.

The overhanging countertop needed to be supported at its deepest point, so I made a pair of brackets.

Done!

Christensen Kitchen

This kitchen is one of my favorites. It had been untouched since undergoing a half-hearted remodel about 30 years ago, and the owners were up for a large-scale structural undertaking, so we knew that the results would be stunning. It also illustrates how some projects have a way of escalating beyond your expectations, becoming more complicated, more time-consuming and more expensive. Be forewarned!

The space had been divided up oddly in the past, so the owners wanted to remove a wall and open up the space. As they were both structural engineers, they were able to handle the technical calculations involved with removing the wall and providing adequate support in its place through the addition of a beam with a vertical column at each end. This turned out to be just the beginning. Once their contractor had torn into the project, they discovered that the exterior wall was woefully inadequate for its load. This required that it be removed and reconstructed, which required a new footing to be poured. The new wall was a perfect match to the existing brick on the exterior of the 100-year-old house, but it certainly added an unforeseen expense.

Once the structural work was done, we were able to stand in the completed space and flesh out the design ideas that we had been tossing around on paper for months. We found that we needed a different arrangement of cabinets along the west wall than we had planned, so it was fortunate that we had decided to hold off building the cabinets until that point.

In terms of the layout, I would describe this as basically a U-shaped layout. The cabinetry does not continuously run on both arms of the "U", but the general functioning of the kitchen does follow that shape. The major muscle of the kitchen is situated galley-style along the west wall — the stove, sink and dishwasher are all clustered here. The north wall features a nice prep area with pull-out trash and recycling containers in the base cabinet. Knives, cutting boards and other kitchen gadgets used for food prep are all located here. The refrigerator is stationed on the south wall. This arrangement makes a convenient work triangle — or work diamond — if you consider the prep area as a fourth station. On the east wall is a showpiece cabinet that was conceived to store dishes and collectibles and also provide serving space for buffet-style dining. This is not a "working area" per se, but it does add to the charm and functional integrity of the kitchen as a whole.

Visually, we were after a traditional look that would be at home in a 100-year-old Victorian-style house that is full of period details both inside and outside. Therefore, we chose a raised-panel door style, turned columns, furniture-style feet and rope moulding to create a classically ornate look. The door and drawer pulls were traditional shapes (cups on the drawers) with a rubbed bronze finish that contrasted well with the cabinets. The appliances were stainless steel, which didn't seem to compete with the traditional cabinetry one bit.

The wall color was a bold, saturated orange-brown color that provided the perfect backdrop for white cabinetry that will look great for years to come. The finish on the cabinets was not paint, but a tinted lacquer that I sprayed at my shop. This finish is extremely durable and easy to maintain.

The hood fan above the stove vented in the outside wall (as compared to the models that simply recirculate the air within the room). The contractor routed the ductwork through the ceiling instead of the back wall, so this required me to construct a chimney to conceal the ductwork between the cabinet and the ceiling. We decided to integrate this chimney into the design by wrapping it with the crown moulding that was installed at the wall-ceiling interface. It worked very well.

In terms of circulation, this room was and is a major hub for the rest of the house. We felt the traffic flow already worked smoothly, so we didn't move any doorways or otherwise restructure the layout of the ancillary spaces.

Another nice attribute of this remodel was the addition of a floor-to-ceiling pantry cabinet next to the kitchen. This is a great way to make use of borrowed space, and its versatile location allows it to be useful for storing kitchen-related items and other things. The homeowners set up a recharging station inside so that chargers and batteries can be maintained while concealing the cords and clutter.

APPLIANCE SAVVY

My clients chose a drawer-style dishwasher. Only two people live in the home and large loads of dishes take time to accumulate, meaning there were longer periods without using the dishwasher. This model dishwasher allows half-loads to be washed, which uses less water and quickly gets dirty dishes back into circulation.

There was already a window in this spot, but that was about the only thing we didn't change during the remodel. The sink and dishwasher were both relocated to the west wall.

A previous remodel provided neither the best possible layout of workspace or storage. An update was certainly in order that included removing the wall behind this cabinetry.

We moved the oven across the room and transformed this area from a workstation into a serving, storage and display area.

The contractor needed to punch a few holes to see where plumbing lines were located. This spot was due to be drywalled anyway.

The last remodel had built a small half-bath and an odd little nook that wasn't well-integrated into the kitchen. The general contractor removed this wall and unified these awkward spaces into one large room.

I used a slot-cutting bit in my router table to cut the stopped grooves in the door stiles and rails.

I cut the bevels on the cabinet door panels using my table saw.

The doors went together with yellow glue.

▶ I built a large, furniture-style piece for the east wall.

▼ I've become a huge fan of the Domino joiner. It provides a fast way to make extremely strong joints.

I used ³/₄" wide masking tape to mock up the placement of the mullions on the cabinet doors. Drawing it out on paper seemed too abstract, and, this method allowed my clients to see the proportions I had in mind.

More than they bargained for: Brand new brick walls had to be erected in the kitchen for structural reasons.

Sometimes it gets worse before it gets better.

Once it was gutted, the small half-bath could be absorbed into the kitchen's new footprint.

Because I had pre-assembled this whole unit in the shop, it was a snap to repeat the process on site. The cleats on the sides of the tall cabinets allowed one person to easily set the center cabinet in place.

▲ All of the cabinets were fastened to the studs in the back wall with long screws.

▲ The plumbing for the sink required holes to be cut in the back of the cabinet. The duct didn't pose a problem, as the sink base cabinet was elevated 4½" above the floor on furniture-style feet.

◄ We installed turned legs at a few key points. In this situation, we needed to secure corresponding spacers to keep the cabinets properly aligned.

◀ The unit came together quickly.

▼ The brand new hardwood floors were in gorgeous shape when we arrived, and careful use of drop cloths assured that they stayed that way.

◀ Cabinet jacks are a necessity for setting upper cabinets in place. I began by centering the cabinet above the stove.

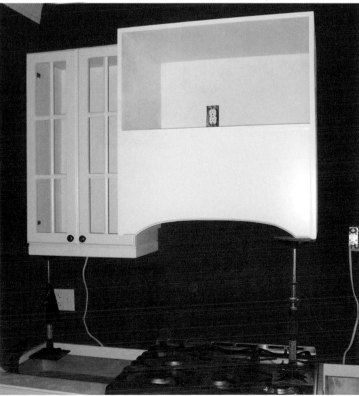

▲ Careful measuring onsite allowed me to pre-cut and assemble the crown moulding in the shop. Its an unusual approach but it worked out great.

▲ The leg on the right-hand side of the dishwasher needed to be boxed in so that it mirrored the one on the opposing side. I built the assembly in the shop and installed it as a completed object.

▶ With the crown in place and the cabinets set, the job was nearly completed. The countertop specialists had been in to make their templates, and within a week or so, the project would be completely finished.

The kitchen turned out looking and functioning very well. The contrast of colors and mixing of construction materials helps things fit into the Victorian house.

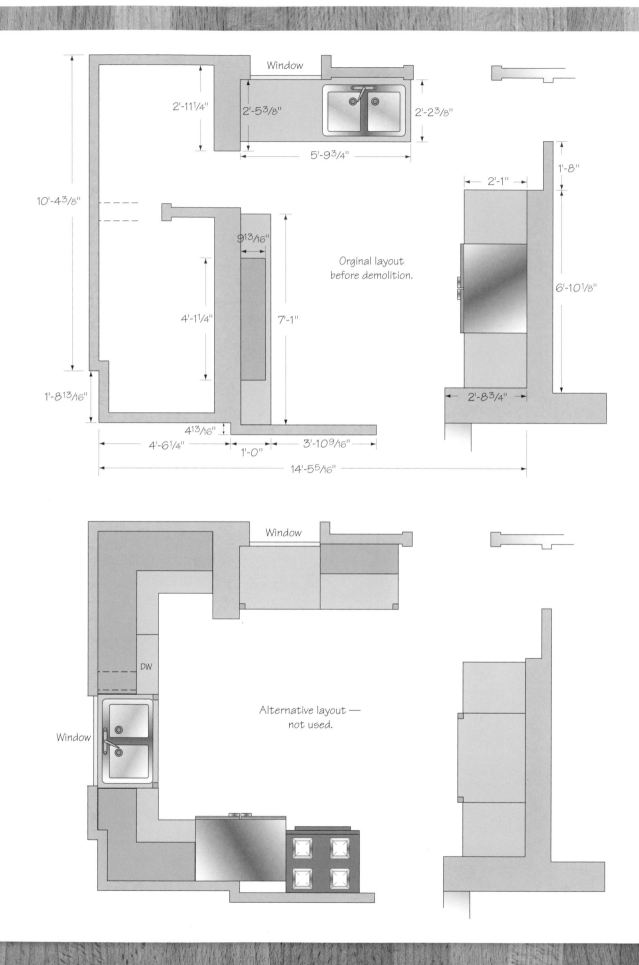

Window

2'-11¹/₄"

2'-5³/₈"

2'-2³/₈"

5'-9³/₄"

2'-1"

1'-8"

10'-4³/₈"

9¹³/₁₆"

Orginal layout
before demolition.

4'-1¹/₄"

7'-1"

6'-10¹/₈"

1'-8¹³/₁₆"

4¹³/₁₆"

4'-6¹/₄"

1'-0"

3'-10⁹/₁₆"

2'-8³/₄"

14'-5⁵/₁₆"

Window

DW

Alternative layout —
not used.

Window

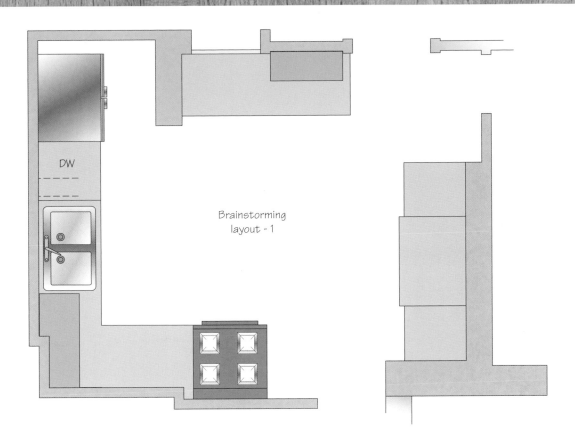

Brainstorming
layout - 1

Original concept layout — not used.

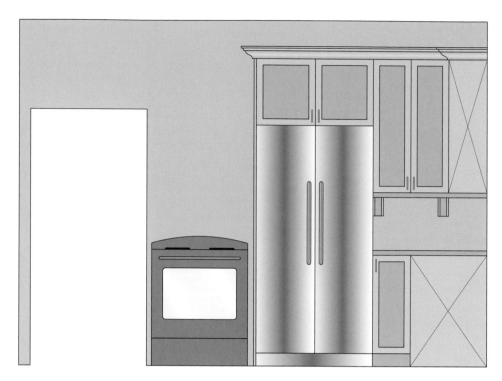

Alternative layout — not used.

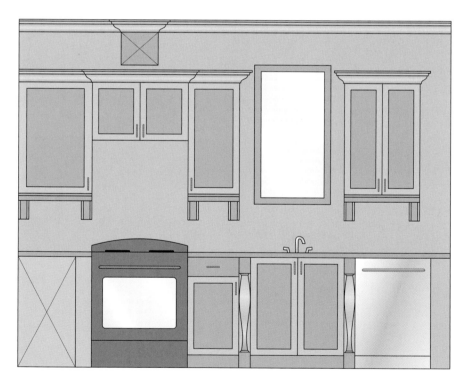

Final concept — used.

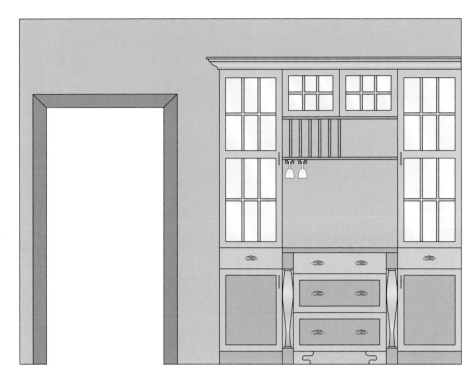

Final concept — used.

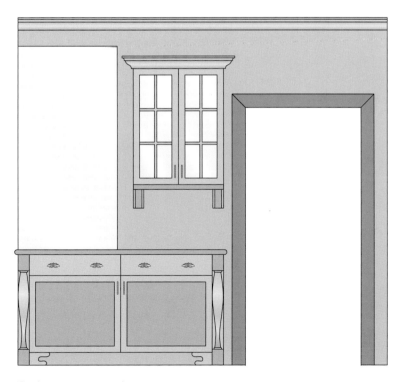

Final concept — used.

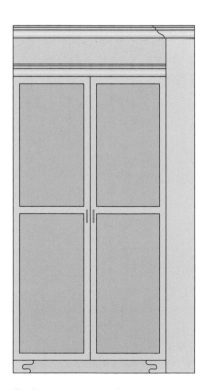

Final concept — used.

Bohner Kitchen

This remodel centered around updating an out-moded kitchen in a 1920's bungalow in the historic Avenues neighborhood in Salt Lake City. The home features many classic elements of bungalow design, but prior to the new owners moving in, it had been a student rental property for decades. As such, it had suffered from years of deferred maintenance, and, although structurally sound, it was ready for a facelift. The homeowners were eager to gain functionality in the kitchen and to make the space brighter and more open.

While the kitchen isn't huge by today's standards, the home features 9'- tall ceilings throughout, which adds quite a nice feeling of openness. Unfortunately, an unknown remodeler had installed some soffits above the sink and the stove (for no apparent reason that I could figure out) and a proper renovation required removing them. This necessitated a bit of

work patching and repairing the existing drywall, but it was worth it. Getting rid of the soffits allowed us to put in cabinets that stretched all the way to the ceiling to take maximum advantage of the available storage space. Using glass-panel doors in the upper cabinets allowed us to retain a bright, open feeling that we were striving for in the project's design.

We didn't move either the plumbing or the electrical wiring, which helped to keep the cost reasonable, but we did move the fridge onto the main wall so that it is in-line with the cabinetry. It had previously been located across the room where it felt like a bit of an obstacle to traffic flow, which was important, because three doorways enter into this kitchen and it is a real hub for movement as people go about their days in the home. We also discarded the non-working dishwasher and installed its replacement to the right of the sink. The layout is a classic L-shape, and while it doesn't offer a ton of built-in counter space, the room was large enough for the homeowners to position a movable workstation across from the sink to make a convenient work area.

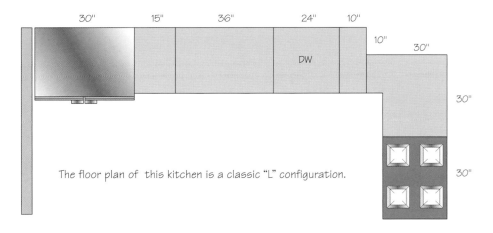

The floor plan of this kitchen is a classic "L" configuration.

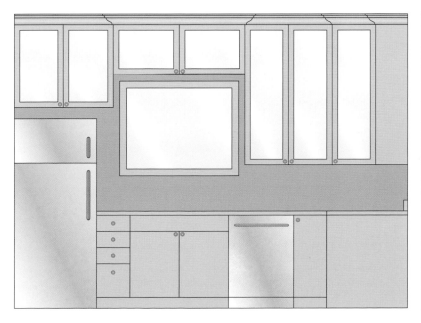

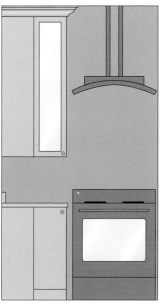

I've been in a lot of kitchens where a previous remodeler had decided to put in some soffits for aesthetic reasons, but I've never seen a situation where it looked nice. It is one thing to build a soffit to hide heating ducts or something like that, but that was not the case here — they were just big, hollow boxes and they had to go. This kitchen featured tall (9') ceilings and it was our goal to take advantage of this fact and help the space to feel brighter and more open.

The soffit came down so far that it cut right across the casing on the top of the window — who thought this looked good?

The electrical wiring below the sink was a bit of a rat's nest.

Sometimes it gets worse before it gets better.

No wonder it always seemed cold in the kitchen. This gap was nearly an inch wide and was "insulated" by a thin layer of plaster.

I cut out the soffit in pieces of a manageable size, which was more civilized than the "smash it to bits" method of demolition that some folks prefer. It came out quickly with a minimal amount of mess.

Once the soffits were removed, the repair to the walls and ceiling was straightforward. I cut new pieces of drywall to fit into the gaps and mudded and taped the seams.

When the wall repair was at a point where I was waiting for the joint compound to dry, I started leveling the bases for the cabinets. This kept things moving along and it was exciting to finally see the new cabinets getting put in place.

Once the cabinet bases had been leveled and secured to the walls, the cabinet could be set in place. Level bases should mean level cabinets, but double-checking with a level never hurts.

Having appliances on hand is always nice, just to make sure that everything will fit as planned.

The interior of the new sink base cabinet is much more orderly than the old one. The outlet was screwed to the wall to provide a place to plug in the dishwasher.

After installing the base cabinets in this kitchen, I brought in some ¾" plywood from the shop so I could make temporary countertops for my clients to use while they waited for their countertop fabricators to finish up their solid-surface tops. This is an easy task that allows the kitchen to become useful again as soon as possible. These tops weren't pretty, but they at least provided a worksurface at a convenient height, and in this case, I re-installed the old sink, which helped out a lot — doing dishes in the bathroom sink gets old really quickly — and we were able to keep that kind of disruption to a minimum. In this case, I disconnected the old sink on Monday morning and began the demolition, and these temporary tops (with the old sink back in action) were in place by Tuesday night. The countertop fabricators weren't scheduled to come until Friday, and they would need at least 10 days after that before they'd be ready to install, so you can see that these temporary tops, allowed my clients to get almost back to normal a full two weeks earlier than they would have otherwise.

This strategy also provided the added bonus of giving me a nice level platform to place my cabinet jacks on when it was time to hang the upper cabinets.

▲ Before I got these cabinet jacks, I used to stack up milk crates, scrap wood and shims to hold cabinets in position. That method works, but it is slower and more awkward. If you have a number of cabinets, you might consider buying some jacks. They are strong, lightweight and easy to adjust. To find them, go to www.fastcap.com.

▶ You'll notice that the back wall has a bump out, which means that the two cabinet shown wouldn't line up to produce a flush front edge. I could have built cabinets of varying depths to compensate for this, but that would have resulted in either a left-handed cabinet that was too deep or a right-handed cabinet that was too shallow. I decided to build cabinets which provided an optimal amount of space. I ended up breaking up the front plane of the cabinetry, which worked out very well.

Because of the different depths of the cabinets, I had to make a lot of cuts in the crown moulding. The results made for a more interesting line of cabinets.

The ensure that the cabinets would line up, I made filler strips to fit between them. Once caulked and painted, the joints disappeared and created a seamless appearance.

Broadmoor Kitchen

This homeowner did an extensive renovation — a complete tear out of a dated 1970's kitchen. They also opened up the space into one large room, eliminating a non-load-bearing wall that used to separate the kitchen from the dining room. I was called in after most of the structural work was done, so the photos for this chapter document the installation of the cabinetry.

The design of the cabinetry was largely inspired by a "wishlist" photo that the homeowner found in a magazine. I find that this happens once in a while in my cabinetry business. Sometimes clients come in with a very specific idea of what they're looking for, and the question then is how to adapt it to their unique situation and address their needs while remaining true to the general look and feel of the original house design. In this case, we had quite a bit of latitude, because we were walking into a space that was so big and open. It made sense to nestle the cabinetry into the back corner and then pull out a peninsula with seating on the opposite side — a classic example of the U-shaped layout.

A key attribute of this design is its overall sleekness. There are no unnecessary drawer or door pulls (we planned for integrated handles cut into the tops of doors and drawers) and the appliances were given as much of a built-in feel as we could create. This meant custom panels for the refrigerator and the use of a built-in wall oven instead of a free-standing range, which would not have contributed to the minimalist look that we were striving for. Because the impact of this design is achieved through simplicity- the massing of the volumes and the elimination of clutter, the remaining design choice become important. The walnut, therefore was chosen as a strong contrast to the glossy white cabinets, and it was laid out horizontally across all of the cabinets. This worked out great, and running the grain continuously was a very important factor. Keeping the grain flowing across the drawer fronts and doors lends a smooth, harmonious feel to the project, and failing to do so would be quite jarring visually. If you choose to do something similar in a project of your own, you'll need to make sure to work within the limitations of the material. Walnut veneers such as these are seldom available in lengths greater than 10', so trying for a continuous run longer than this could be difficult if not impossible. We didn't need to go more than 8', so we were able to use the locally available 4×8 sheets of plywood carried by my lumberyard of choice.

For maximum durability, I chose a tinted lacquer for the glossy white finish on the cabinets. I applied it with an HVLP sprayer, and it went down flawlessly and quickly. It will also be very easy to clean.

The old tile flooring was removed and a new hardwood floor was installed. Also, new windows and sliding doors were installed for a greater connection with the outside, better views and more natural light.

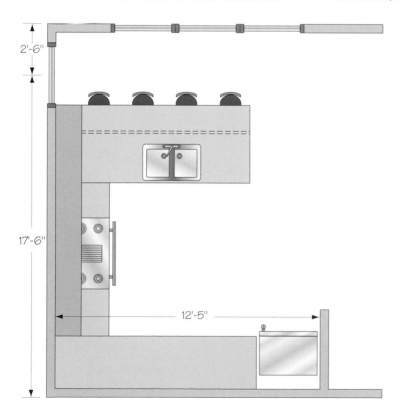

It is nice to walk into a clean job site that is ready for cabinets — it makes the process go a lot more smoothly.

We began the installation by bringing all of the various components in and setting them in approximately their final positions. It was easy to fine tune their fits once we had a "rough draft" set up.

The cabinets needed to be screwed together in ways that wouldn't be visible later on. For these base units, that meant removing the drawers temporarily.

The inside corner between the stove wall and the peninsula required an L-shaped filler so the drawers and doors would have enough clearance to operate properly. Because I had taken the time to pre-assemble this project in the shop, I knew this filler would work. All I had to do was screw it in place.

I attached the filler strip to the cabinets with L-brackets.

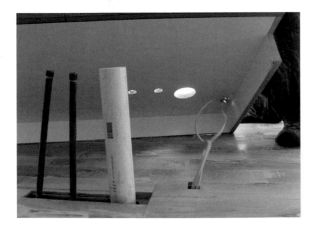

Because the sink is located on a peninsula rather than along a wall, the plumbing had to be run through the floor. Once we were on site, I drilled the necessary holes and dropped the cabinet into place. Note the electrical line that services the dishwasher.

I build a lot of peninsulas, and this is one of my favorite techniques for utilizing all of the available storage space: A corner cabinet that faces out. Nobody likes storage that is accessed from an inside corner, because it can be hard to reach, but when you turn the cabinet around, you have complete access to it. It is also a simpler and less expensive cabinet than a traditional corner cabinet with a lazy Susan.

I cut the doors out from the same sheet that I used for the back of this island so the grain was continuous. Note the transition from the doors to the toe kick is uninterrupted to keep the look as clean as possible.

Once the bases were set, I raised the upper units on cabinet jacks. After checking their position with a level, I screwed them to the studs in the wall using 3" washer-head screws.

Here's a glimpse part-way through the install.

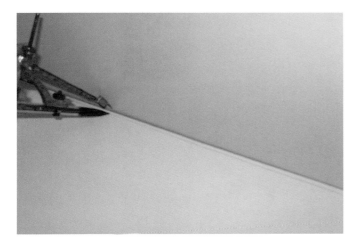

The homeowners chose a white laminate countertop with a walnut front edge. The top needed to be scribed along the back wall. Using a compass, I traced the profile of the wall onto the back edge of the top and trimmed it along this line.

The sink was an undermount, which meant that the edge of the countertop would be visible on the cutout. To accommodate this, I added some walnut boards into the subtop. This took some planning and a bit of extra time, but it was worth it. To protect the wood, I sealed it with spar varnish after the cutout was made using the template included by the sink manufacturer.

The sink attached to the bottom of the subtop with some pieces of hardware provided by the manufacturer.

The cooktop didn't come with a template, so I measured the unit and cut an opening in the countertop.

A perfect fit.

The hood fan needed to be centered above the cooktop so it would draft properly. Fortunately we had planned for this and built a mini-panel to attach the door-lifting mechanism to. Had I attached the lifter to a full-size panel, it would have been in the way of the fan. The fan was used in the "recirculate" mode so it didn't matter if the opening for the ductwork was less accessible.

From below, the fan is clean and simple.

To give the fridge a built-in look, I made panels the sizes specified by the manufacturer and finished them to match the other components. Once the panel is in place, a small cap covers the top edge so it is finished all the way around.

To coordinate with the sleek look of the kitchen, we chose door lifters that allow the doors to be raised with the flick of a wrist. They were easy to install and adjust, but they are expensive — nearly $200 per door.

I built a box to conceal the fan motor. It can be easily removed if necessary.

This photo shows how the grain ran continuously across all the drawer fronts on the stove wall. This dishwasher had to be returned because it could not accept a front panel, and the homeowner really wanted its front to be trimmed in walnut.

The hardware is called a "parallel lift system" for obvious reasons. I like the hardware (except for the price) but there's something that should be pointed out — the mechanisms are big. When the doors are in the closed position, the metal arms extend almost from top to bottom inside the cabinets, so the shelves can't be as deep as they would usually be. Not a deal-breaker, but this would have been good to know beforehand.

The drawers were deep, and they were mounted on full-extension runners to provide the best possible access to their contents.

Thinking Beyond the Kitchen: Incorporating Adjacent Spaces

A kitchen trend that I'm seeing involves transforming an area near the kitchen to enhance the entire dining experience. This can take many forms. Not all of us have the space to dedicate to a classic butler's pantry, but I've seen a few cases where hallway space was developed into a first-rate storage and work area.

The kitchen was rather small and couldn't be expanded without blowing the budget, but we found a great opportunity to improve the overall functionality. Between the kitchen and dining room, a large pre-existing niche seemed like an ideal place to situate a piece that would provide storage and maybe even some light-duty workspace. We knew from the beginning that we would keep the materials and finishes the same as in the kitchen to foster the impression that the kitchen is larger than it is.

We started with the idea of emulating an old Hoosier-style cabinet, but we couldn't find a way to get enough storage while staying true to the historic attributes of the Hoosier form. We continued to entertain ideas for a furniture piece which would offer the advantage of portability, so the owners could take it with them if they moved. In the end we decided on a furniture-style built-in. It would sacrifice the advantage of portability but on the other hand, it became a part of the home and would certainly add to its resale value.

We began the planning process by assessing the current kitchen's weaknesses and creating a wishlist of ideas for the project.

CURRENT KITCHEN WEAKNESSES:
- Very limited storage
- Very limited counter space — just enough for prep but not for serving
- Kitchen not directly adjacent to dining area — it's down a hallway — awkward when somebody drops a fork or you need another napkin during the meal
- microwave and toaster in an awkward spot (in a cabinet behind an entry door)
- No place to put coffee maker and leave it out
- No recycling center

WISHLIST FOR THE NEW BUILT-IN:
- Meet the needs not addressed by the current kitchen
- Be a full-service adjutant to the dining room with linen storage, wine glass storage, dishes, flatware
- That it can function as a sideboard to arrange food for serving
- Lighting that is useful for displaying whatever is on the counter (i.e., the Thanksgiving turkey) but also as a part of the overall lighting plan for the room

- Be a major focal point for this part of the house — it is visible from many vantage points
- Butcher block countertops to complement the rustic feel of the home
- A painted finish to contrast with all of the wood everywhere else (it's a log home)
- Some furniture-style elements so that it's more than just a bunch of cabinet boxes
- Maximize counter space

THINGS THAT YOU MAY WISH TO INCORPORATE IN A BUTLER'S PANTRY OR OTHER ANCILLARY SPACE:
- Wet bar
- Liquor storage
- Wine cooler
- Clean-up area with separate dishwasher
- Prep area with cutting boards and knives
- Food storage — particularly if you buy in bulk
- Decorative elements such as a mosaic tile backsplash
- Could be a breakfast bar — this is a potentially very useful application — but would need seating
- Display of dishes or collectibles: Need open shelves or glass doors
- Mini fridge
- A designated "snack station" where kids can help themselves — may incorporate a lower counter
- A built-in stool, maybe a microwave, mini-fridge
- Meal-planning area with cookbooks and a corkboard and/or chalkboard
- Coffee bar

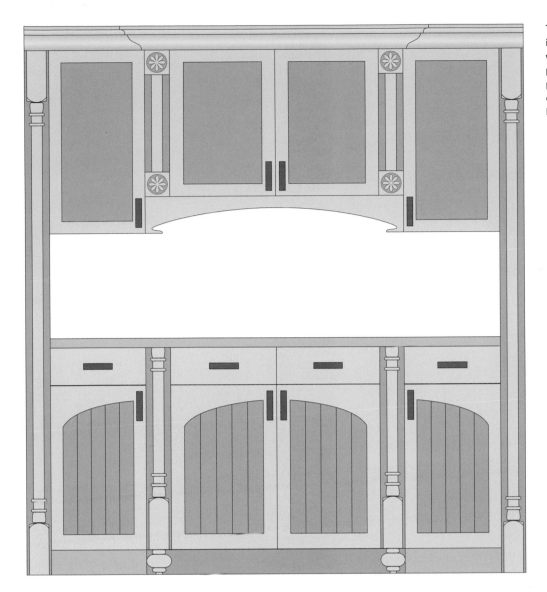

The original sketch/drawing included some elements that weren't included in the final project. One was the two arched-panel outside doors on the base cabinet. For visual reasons, they became square-panel doors.

You'll notice that the finished piece varied slightly from the original sketch: This is because we kept our options open and changed our minds as the piece shaped up. I had initially liked the idea of using arched doors on the ends of the base, but once I built the doors, I found that there was something visually jarring about the interrupted arches on the sides. Rather than contributing a bit of whimsy to the piece, it just didn't work.

The final form for this project was rather unique — I used a top-to-bottom column to provide unity to the composition — I didn't want the piece to read as top and bottom sections but rather as a whole piece. This would've been easy to achieve if the upper cabinets extended downwards to connect with the mass of the bottom section, but alas, we needed the counter space.

Even though the pantry incorporates some formal elements like turned feet and columns,
the goal was not to create a stern, serious piece — by staying flexible throughout the process,
we were able to achieve the goals of our original vision.

SUPPLIERS

**ADAMS & KENNEDY —
THE WOOD SOURCE**
6178 Mitch Owen Rd.
P.O. Box 700
Manotick, ON
Canada K4M 1A6
613-822-6800
www.wood-source.com
Wood supply

B&Q
Portswood House
1 Hampshire Corporate Park
Chandlers Ford
Eastleigh
Hampshire, England SO53
3YX
0845 609 6688
www.diy.com
*Woodworking tools, supplies
and hardware*

BUSY BEE TOOLS
130 Great Gulf Dr.
Concord, ON
Canada L4K 5W1
1-800-461-2879
www.busybeetools.com
*Woodworking tools and
supplies*

CABPARTS. INC.
716 Arrowest Road
Grand Junction, CO 81505
970-241-7682
www.cabparts.com
*Cabinets, drawers, doors, closet
components*

**CONSTANTINE'S WOOD CENTER
OF FLORIDA**
1040 E. Oakland Park Blvd.
Fort Lauderdale, FL 33334
800-443-9667
www.constantines.com
*Tools, woods, veneers,
hardware*

THE CABINET DOOR SHOP
104 Bratton Drive
Hot Springs, Arkansas
71901
800-297-3667
www.cabinetdoorshop.com
*Cabinet doors and drawers,
wainscotting, hardware*

**FRANK PAXTON LUMBER
COMPANY**
5701 W. 66th St.
Chicago, IL 60638
800-323-2203
www.paxtonwood.com
Wood, hardware, tools, books

HARDWARE RESOURCES
Hardware Resources
4319 Marlena St
Bossier City, LA 71111
800-463-0660
www.hardwareresources.
com
*Cabinet hardware, drawer
boxes, cabinet pullouts,
mouldings*

THE HOME DEPOT
2455 Paces Ferry Rd. NW
Atlanta, GA 30339
800-430-3376 (U.S.)
800-628-0525 (Canada)
www.homedepot.com
*Woodworking tools, supplies
and hardware*

KLINGSPOR ABRASIVES INC.
2555 Tate Blvd. SE
Hickory, N.C. 28602
800-645-5555
www.klingspor.com
Sandpaper of all kinds

LEE VALLEY TOOLS LTD.
P.O. Box 1780
Ogdensburg, NY 13669-6780
800-871-8158 (U.S.)
800-267-8767 (Canada)
www.leevalley.com
*Woodworking tools and
hardware*

LOWE'S COMPANIES, INC.
P.O. Box 1111
North Wilkesboro, NC 28656
800-445-6937
www.lowes.com
*Woodworking tools, supplies
and hardware*

OMEGA NATIONAL PRODUCTS
900 Baxter Avenue
P.O. Box 4368
Louisville, KY 40204
502-583-3038
www.omeganationalprod-
ucts.com
Tambour doors and panels

**ROCKLER WOODWORKING AND
HARDWARE**
4365 Willow Dr.
Medina, MN 55340
800-279-4441
www.rockler.com
*Woodworking tools, hardware
and books*

STANISCI DESIGN
14823 32 Mile Rd
Romeo, MI 48065
586-752-3368
www.wood-hood.com
*Wood range hoods, ventilators,
premier wood carvings*

TOOL TREND LTD.
140 Snow Blvd. Unit 1
Concord, ON
Canada L4K 4C1
416-663-8665
*Woodworking tools and
hardware*

**TREND MACHINERY & CUTTING
TOOLS LTD.**
Odhams Trading Estate
St. Albans Rd.
Watford
Hertfordshire, U.K.
WD24 7TR
01923 224657
www.trendmachinery.co.uk
*Woodworking tools and
hardware*

WATERLOX COATINGS
908 Meech Ave.
Cleveland, OH 44105
800-321-0377
www.waterlox.com
Finishing supplies

WESTERN DOVETAIL, INC.
Western Dovetail, Inc.
P.O. Box 1592
Vallejo, CA 94590
800-800-DOVE [3683]
www.drawer.com
*Dovetailed drawers made
to order*

WHITE RIVER HARDWOODS
1197 Happy Hollow Road
Fayetteville, AR 72701
800-558-0119
www.mouldings.com
*Hardwood mouldings,
handcarved architectural
wood carvings*

WOODCRAFT SUPPLY LLC
1177 Rosemar Rd.
P.O. Box 1686
Parkersburg, WV 26102
800-535-4482
www.woodcraft.com
Woodworking hardware

WOODWORKER'S HARDWARE
P.O. Box 180
Sauk Rapids, MN 56379-
0180
800-383-0130
www.wwhardware.com
Woodworking hardware

WOODWORKER'S SUPPLY
1108 N. Glenn Rd.
Casper, WY 82601
800-645-9292
http://woodworker.com
*Woodworking tools and
accessories, finishing supplies,
books and plans*

More great titles from Popular Woodworking and Betterway Home!

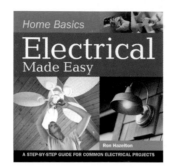

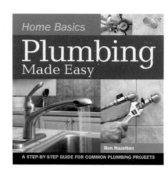

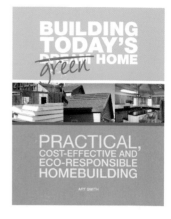

ROOM BY ROOM
by Monte Burch

Room by Room Storage Solutions provides simple, quick storage solutions using readily available and inexpensive storage products to organize every room in the house. Also included are tips on assessing storage needs, organizing for easy storage and efficient use as well as tips on staying organized. This helpful guide makes organized storage easy by giving time-saving ideas for using readily available (and inexpensive) storage products.

ISBN 13: 978-1-55870-870-9
ISBN 10: 1-55870-870-7,
paperback, 144 p., #Z3007

**HOME BASICS:
ELECTRICAL MADE EASY**
by Ron Hazelton

Author Ron Hazelton walks you, step-by-step, through the most basic and most common electrical projects all homeowners will encounter. Projects include:
• Adding a new outlet or switch
• Install low-voltage outdoor lighting
• Replacing a light fixture
• Install a programmable thermostat
• Install a ceiling fan

ISBN 13: 978-1-55870-896-9
ISBN 10: 1-55870-896-0,
hardcover w/wiro, 240 p., #Z4271

**HOME BASICS:
PLUMBING MADE EASY**
by Ron Hazelton

Author Ron Hazelton walks you, step-by-step, through the most basic and most common plumbing projects all homeowners will encounter. Projects include:
• Protecting pipes from freezing
• Perfect caulk application
• Replacing a faucet
• Replacing a dishwasher
• Repair a toilet
• Fix a damaged garden hose
• Create a fish pond

ISBN 13: 978-1-55870-898-3
ISBN 10: 1-55870-898-7,
hardcover w/wiro, 240 p., #Z4370

**BUILDING TODAY'S
GREEN HOME**
by Art Smith

Building the right-sized home involves making eco-smart decisions. Learn how to choose the correct location, how to design the right-sized home for your needs, what are the best sustainable materials, what HVAC units are the most effective and how to grade the lot for natural sustainability.

ISBN 13: 978-1-55870-862-4
ISBN 10: 1-55870-862-6,
paperback, 160 p., #Z2843

These and other great woodworking books are available at your local bookstore, woodworking stores or from online suppliers.

www.popularwoodworking.com